John Richard Burton

A History of Bewdley

With concise accounts of some neighbouring parishes

John Richard Burton

A History of Bewdley
With concise accounts of some neighbouring parishes

ISBN/EAN: 9783337429072

Printed in Europe, USA, Canada, Australia, Japan

Cover: Foto ©ninafisch / pixelio.de

More available books at **www.hansebooks.com**

A

HISTORY OF BEWDLEY;

WITH CONCISE ACCOUNTS OF SOME NEIGHBOURING PARISHES.

BY JOHN R. BURTON, B.A., F.G.S.,

RECTOR OF DOWLES.

LONDON:

PUBLISHED FOR THE AUTHOR BY WILLIAM REEVES,

185, FLEET STREET, E.C.

1883.

TO

William Nichols Marcy, Esquire,

LORD OF THE MANOR OF BEWDLEY,

THIS ATTEMPT TO ILLUSTRATE

THE HISTORY OF

THE ANCIENT BOROUGH

IS INSCRIBED.

PREFACE.

THIS work has been drawn from very many sources. The Corporation Records were kindly placed at my disposal by R. Hemingway, Esq., Town Clerk. For permission to examine the voluminous MSS. of Dr. Prattinton in the Society of Antiquaries I am indebted to C. Knight Watson, Esq. The Hayley MSS. were lent me by the Rev. John Cawood; and the Ribbesford Registers by the Rev. E. H. Winnington Ingram. My thanks are also due to the Rev. J. E. A. Fenwick for access to several rare books in the fine library collected by the late Sir Thos. Phillipps, Bart., at Thirlestaine House, Cheltenham. Help has likewise been kindly given in various ways by the Bishop of Worcester, the Dean of Worcester, J. O. Halliwell-Phillipps, Esq., LL.D., F.R.S., Professor Willis-Bund, Rev. A. James, Rev. E. Bradley ("Cuthbert Bede"), Rev. J. P. Hastings, S. Z. Lloyd, Esq., and many others.

The materials for this work have been accumulating for several years, and would make a far larger book than that now laid before the reader. A local history can, however, only expect a limited circulation; and it was not considered desirable to increase the price first named.

The account of Stourport and the villages adjoining Bewdley does not claim to be more than a mere outline. A New County History, which is to be taken in hand shortly, will most likely do ample justice to these places.

Any profits there may be from the sale of this book will be given for the benefit of Dowles Church and Sunday School.

BEWDLEY, *June*, 1883. J. R. B.

LIST OF SUBSCRIBERS.

Alderson, Rev. Frank, Dudleston Vicarage, Ellesmere.
Andrews, Mr. W., F.R.H.S., Hull.
Antiquaries, Society of, Burlington House, London.

Bagster, Mr. Basil B., Wribbenhall. (4 copies.)
Bagster, Mr. Henry T., Wribbenhall.
Baker, Mr. George, Beaucastle, Bewdley.
Baker, Mr. Richard C., Wribbenhall.
Baker, Mr. Slade, Sandbourne.
Baldwin, Mr. Alfred, Wilden House.
Baldwin, Mr. Enoch, M.P., The Mount, Stourport. (3 copies.)
Baldwyn, Mr. J. Gough, Stourport.
Bancks, Mrs. C. P., Bewdley.
Bancks, Miss, Wribbenhall.
Barton, Mr. Everard, Summerdine. (2 copies.)
Barton, Mr. William, Stamford.
Bathe, Rev. S. B., St. George's Vicarage, Kidderminster.
Baugh, Mrs., Bewdley. (2 copies.)
Beaman, Mr. John, Bewdley. (2 copies.)
Beauchamp, Right Hon. the Earl, Madresfield Court. (2 copies.)
Beddoe, Mr. Henry C., Hereford.
Beddoe, John, M.D., F.R.S., Bristol.
Beeby, Mrs. R., Stoke Golding.
Belling, Mr. John, M.A., Stonehouse.
Bentley, Rev. S., Bosbury Vicarage.
Birmingham Free Library.
Blencowe, Rev. Alfred J., Witton Vicarage, Northwich.
Blencowe, Rev. Charles E., Marston Vicarage, Banbury.
Blencowe, Mr. John A., Marston House.
Blencowe, Miss, Marston House.
Booth, Mrs., Wribbenhall.
Boraston, Miss, Dublin. (3 copies.)
Boraston, Mr. S., Wribbenhall.
Boughton, Sir Charles Rouse, Bart., Downton Hall, Ludlow. (3 copies.)
Bradley, Rev. Edward, Stretton Vicarage, Oakham.
Brinton, Mr. John, M.P., Moor Hall, Stourport.
Bromley, Miss, Bewdley. (3 copies.)
Bury, Mr. John, Kateshill, Bewdley. (2 copies.)

List of Subscribers.

Bury, Miss, Bewdley.
Brown, Mr. Charles, Droitwich.
Bryan, Miss, Bewdley.
Burton, Miss, Paris. (2 copies.)
Burton, Miss, Stamford.
Burton, Mr. George H., Stamford.
Carnarvon, Right Hon. the Earl of, Portman-square, London.
Cartwright, Mrs., Stourport.
Cave, Rev. Fred. L., Bloxham. (2 copies.)
Cawood, Rev. John, Bayton Rectory.
Chellingworth, Mr. W. H., Trimpley House.
Chesshire, Rev. James L., Wribbenhall Vicarage.
Childe, Mrs. E. Baldwyn, Kyre Park, Tenbury.
Clack, Mr. J. S., Bedford.
Claughton, Rev. T. Legh, Vicarage, Kidderminster. (2 copies.)
Clinch, Mr. Alfred M., Bewdley. (4 copies.)
Cole, Miss, Bordesley Hall, Redditch.
Colledge, Mr., Dowles.
Compton, the Very Rev. Lord Alwyne, the Deanery, Worcester.
Cownley, Miss, Kidderminster.
Cooke, Mr. George, Carlisle.
Cooke, Miss, Tettenhall.
Cookes, Rev. H. W., Astley Rectory.
Corbet, Mr. Henry, Fort Royal, Worcester.
Crane, Mr. H., Oakhampton, near Stourport.
Crane, Mrs., Oakhampton, near Stourport.
Crane, Mr. John H., Hillhampton House.
Crane, Miss, Bewdley.
Crowe, Miss, Bewdley.

Dalley, Mr. T. C., Bewdley. (2 copies.)
Davies, Mr. D. Lloyd, Wyre Court, Bewdley.
Davis, Rev. E. V. W., Abdon Rectory.
Davis, Mrs., Dowles.
Daunt, Mr. A. Kingscote, Bewdley.
Dewse, Mr. G., Stamford.
Dingwall, Mr. R. M., Clapham, S.W.
Downing, Mr. J. Marshall, Dowles. (3 copies.)
Dunn, Rev. M. W. M., Sutton Coldfield.

Essington, Mrs., Ribbesford House.

Fenwick, Rev. J. E. A., Thirlestaine House, Cheltenham.
Fisher, Mr. J. B., Wribbenhall.
Fletcher, Mrs., Kingston-on-Thames. (2 copies.)
Fleming, Mrs., Wribbenhall. (3 copies.)
Foley, Right Hon. Lord, Grosvenor-square, London.
Foley, Mr. P. H., Prestwood, Stourbridge.

List of Subscribers.

Ford, Rev. W. O. Parker, the Vicarage, Bewdley.
Foster, Mr. W. O., Apley Park, Bridgnorth.
Foster, Mr. W. J., Bewdley.
Foster, Mrs., Wells.

Gabb, Mr. John, Bewdley. (2 copies.)
Gabb, Mr. Leonard A., Bewdley. (2 copies.)
Gardiner, Mr. Benjamin, Eymore House. (2 copies.)
Gibbons, Rev. B., Waresley House, Hartlebury. (2 copies,)
Godson, Mr. A. F., Pump-court, Temple, E.C.
Grazebrook, Mr. H. Sidney, Chiswick.
Gretton, Rev. F. E., B.D., Oddington Rectory, Stow-on-the-Wold.
Griffin, Mr. G. F., Stourport.
Groome, Mrs., Eastbourne.
Gurney, Rev. A. W., Little Hereford Rectory, Tenbury.

Hall, Lieut. F., R.N., Broadway.
Hall, Miss, Ashford House, Ludlow.
Hallen, Rev. W., Wribbenhall.
Harrison, Mr. C., Areley Court.
Hancocks, Mr. W., Blakeshall House.
Harvey, Mr. James J., Kidderminster.
Hassall, Miss, Wribbenhall.
Hastings, Rev. J. P., Martley Rectory.
Havergal, Rev. Prebendary F. T., Upton Bishop Vicarage.
Hately, Mrs., Clifton.
Haywood, Mr. J. S., Worcester.
Hemingway, Mr. R., Bewdley.
Hereford, Right Rev. the Lord Bishop of, Hereford.
Hereford, the Hon. and Very Rev. the Dean of, Hereford.
Hemming, Mrs. Walter, Spring Grove, Bewdley.
Hill, Mr. T. R., Q.C., M.P., Worcester.
Hinton, Mr. W., Bewdley.
Homfray, Mr. H., Kidderminster.
Hopkins, Mr. T., Bewdley.
Humpherson, Mr. Chas. J., Newport, Monmouthshire. (2 copies.)

Ife, Miss, Melton Mowbray.
Ife, Miss Ellen, London.
Ingram, Rev. E. H. Winnington, Ribbesford Rectory. (4 copies.)
Irving, Rev. Alex., Wellington College. (2 copies.)

James, Rev. Alfred, Burwarton Rectory.
James, Rev. G. Howard, Nottingham.
Jefferies, Mr. C. E., Wribbenhall.

Kane, Mrs., The Grange, Monmouth.
Kenrick, Mr. W., Harborne.
Knight, Mr. F. Wynn, M.P., Wolverley House, Kidderminster.

List of Subscribers.

Lamb, Mr. W. M., Worcester.
Lamb, Miss J., Bewdley.
Landon, Mr. Whittington, Bewdley.
Lawrence, Mr. J. T., Bewdley.
Lea, Rev. Josiah T., Far Forest Vicarage. (2 copies.)
Lea, Mr. John W. T., Netherton House, Bewdley.
Lea, Ven. Archdeacon, St. Peter's Vicarage, Droitwich.
Lea, Rev. F. Simcox, Tedstone Delamere Rectory, Worcester.
Lechmere, Sir Edw. A., Bart., M.P., Rhydd Court, Upton-on-Severn.
Lloyd, Mr. S. Zachary, Areley Hall, Stourport.
London Library, 12, St. James'-square, S.W.
Lubbock, Sir John, Bart., M.P., Lombard-street, E.C.
Lyttelton, the Right Hon. Lord, Hagley Hall, Stourbridge.
Lyttelton, the Hon. and Rev. Canon, Hagley Rectory.
Lyttelton, the Hon. and Rev. Arthur T., Selwyn College, Cambridge.

McClelland, Mr. Hugh, Birmingham.
Manby, Mr. Cordy, Wassall Wood, Bewdley. (2 copies.)
Manchester, Right Rev. the Lord Bishop of
Marcy, Mr. W. Nichols, Manor House, Bewdley. (8 copies.)
Marcy, Mrs. ditto ditto.
Martin, Mr. Joseph, Stourport.
Moilliet, Rev. J. L., Abberley Rectory, Stourport. (2 copies.)
Monck, Rev. Edward, Battle, Sussex.
Moore, Miss, Liverpool.
Morrall, Mr. E., Bridgnorth.
Morris, Rev. Haywood, Stottesdon Vicarage.
Morris, Mr. T., Hereford.
Morris, Mr., Stourbridge.
Morton, Mr. E. J., Wolverley.

Nellist, Mr., Crundalls, Wribbenhall.
Nicholas, Mrs., Malvern.
Nicholas, Mr. Richmond, Wimbledon, Surrey. (3 copies.)
Nicholas, Miss, Wribbenhall.
Nicholls, Mr. John, Bewdley.
Nicholson, Mr. T., F.I.B.A., Hereford.
Norris, Mr. W., The Mount, Tenbury.
North, Mr. Thos., F.S.A., Llanfairfechan.

Ouseley, Rev. Sir Fred. A. G., Bart., St. Michael's College, Tenbury.
Owens, Mr. Thos., Bewdley.

Parkes, Miss, Blakebrook, Kidderminster.
Parton, Mr. W., Wribbenhall.
Payne, Mr. Philip, Bewdley.
Pease, Mr. Arthur, M.P., Darlington.
Pease, Miss Beatrice, Darlington.

List of Subscribers.

Pease, Sir Joseph W., Bart., M.P., Guisbro' Hall, Yorkshire.
Pemberton, Mr. Geo. A., Dowles.
Phillipps, Mr. J. O. Halliwell, F.R.S , Hollingbury Copse, Sussex.
Phillipps, Miss K. E. Halliwell, Hollingbury Copse.
Philipps, Mrs., Edgbaston.
Pitt, Miss Harriet, Wribbenhall.
Player, Mr. J. Hort, Birmingham. (3 copies.)
Pountney, Mr. Charles, Bewdley.
Powis, Right Hon. Earl of, Powis Castle, Welshpool.
Prescott, Mrs., Birches Farm, Tenbury.
Price, Mr. S., Bewdley.
Puckey, Mr. J. C., Stansted, Essex.
Purton, Rev. John, Oldbury Rectory, Bridgnorth.

Rayson, Rev. William, R.D., Lindridge Vicarage.
Reiss, Rev. Fred. A., Rock Rectory. (2 copies.)
Reiss, Mrs. L., 22, Princes-gate, London.
Roberts, Mr. T. Lloyd, Corfton Manor, Shropshire. (2 copies.)
Robertson, Rev. David, R.D., Hartlebury Rectory. (2 copies.)
Rollason, Mr. T., Handsworth.
Rushout, the Hon Miss, Burford House, Tenbury.

Salisbury, Very Rev. the Dean of, Salisbury.
St. Albans, Right Rev. the Lord Bishop of, Danbury Palace. (3 copies.)
Sanders, Rev. S. J. W., Northampton.
Shaw, Mr. Giles, Winterdyne. (3 copies.)
Smith, Mr. James, Bewdley.
Smith, Mr. John, Bewdley.
Smith, Rev. Prebendary I. G., the Vicarage, Malvern.
Smith, Mr. S., Public Library and Museum, Worcester.
Smith, Rev. T. Ayscough, the Vicarage, Tenbury.
Southwell, Mr. T. Martin, Bridgnorth.
Spencer, Mr. W. F., Spring Grove.
Stone, Mr. James E., Kidderminster.
Sturge, Mr. Charles, Wribbenhall. (4 copies.)
Swinburn, Mrs., Wribbenhall.

Tangye, Mr. Joseph, Ticknell.
Tempest-Radford, Mr. T., Kidderminster.
Temple, Sir Richard, Bart., G.C.S.I., the Nash, Kempsey.
Tomkinson, Mr. M., Kidderminster.
Tonks, Mr. J., Bewdley.
Turner, Rev. G. P., Downton Vicarage, Ludlow.

Vawdrey, Rev. Daniel, Areley Kings Rectory.

Walcot, Rev. John, Bitterley Court, Ludlow.
Walcot, Mrs. Owen, the Erwy, near Ellesmere.

List of Subscribers.

Walcot, Commander John C. P., R.N., Bitterley.
Walcot, John Halliwell, the Erwy.
Warner, Rev. Prebendary C., Clun Rectory. (2 copies.)
Watson, Mr. John, Waresley.
Watson, Mr. C. Hugh, Stourport.
Webster, Mr. Cecil, Bewdley.
Whieldon, Rev. Edward, Hales Hall, Cheadle. (3 copies.)
Whitcombe, Mr. R. H., Bewdley.
White, Mr. Milson, Bewdley.
White, Mrs. R., Upton-on-Severn.
Wilding, Rev. C. J., Arley Vicarage.
Willis-Bund, Mr. J. W., Wick Episcopi, near Worcester.
Wilson, Mr. Geo. E., Wyddrington, Birmingham. (2 copies.)
Windsor-Clive, Lady Mary, Oakley Park. (2 copies.)
Winnington, the Dowager Lady, Ashburton House, Putney.
Wodehouse Mrs., Ham Hill, Worcester.
Wood, Mr. E. T. W., Henley Hall, Ludlow.
Woodward, Mr. Robert, Arley Castle. (2 copies.)
Woodward, Mr. Robert, jun., Arley Cottage.
Woodward Mrs., Ashdown Cottage, Tenbury.
Woodward, Mr. H. Toye, Kidderminster.
Worcester, Right Rev. Lord Bishop of, Hartlebury Castle.

CONTENTS.

CORRIGENDA.

Page 9, line 2 from bottom: for *roll* read *toll*.

Page 13, ,, 2 ,, : insert 18.

Page 61, ,, 12 ,, : Sam. Skey the *elder* was buried April 4, 1800.

Page 64, ,, 2 ,, : for *at* read *ad*.

Page xxix., line 7: for *Tuckers* read *Tinkers*.

Page xli., line 3 from bottom: for 1883 read 1835.

Rise of the Town and Descent of the Manor.

HE earliest mention of the modern Bewdley occurs under its old Saxon name of Wribbenhall—a name still retained by the adjacent village on the eastern side of the Severn. In the time of William the Conqueror both formed part of the great manor of Kidderminster. We read in Domesday Book (1085):—"King William holds in demesne Chideminstre, with sixteen berewicks or hamlets: Wenvertun, Trimpelei, Worcote, Frenesse (Franche), and another Frenesse, Bristitune, Harburgelei (Habberley), Fastochesfelde, Gurbehale, Ribeford, and another Ribeford, Sudtone, Aldintone, Metune (Mitton), Tuelesberge, Sudwale. In these lands together with the manor are twenty hides*: the manor was all waste." The name *Gurbehale* here mentioned is no doubt the Norman way of spelling Wribbenhall; for having no letter *W*, the Normans expressed the sound by "Gu"—*e.g.*, Gulielmus for Willelmus, Gualterus for Walterus, Guarrena for Warrena. By substituting *W* for "Gu" we get Wrbehale; and we find it thus written in the annals of the Church of Worcester:—"In the year 1215 Hugh de Mortimer did fealty for Wrbehale in the

* A Domesday "Hide" was about 240 acres.

Chapter-house at Worcester of 20s. a year, which his predecessors had granted to the said church to be received by the hands of certain persons; who, because they would not render their rent, being ejected, both for a valuable consideration and by force, he himself took the said land, and was to render the rent."* The Register of the Priory of St. Mary of Worcester (1240) informs us how Wribbenhall first came into the possession of the Church, and reads thus:—"*Concerning Wrubenhale.* A certain man, Thurstin by name, gave us Wrubenhal, Ralph de Mortimer senior conceding and confirming, as his charter beareth witness. In after times Roger de Mortimer took it for a fief. Whence he swore fealty to the Prior and Convent, and gave a relief [payment to the lord by a feudal tenant on entering his fief], and bound his heirs, as his charter witnesseth, to do fealty to the Prior and Convent, and to give a relief according to circumstances, and to pay every year at the feast of St. Martin twenty shillings."†

The charter of Thurstin or Turstin here mentioned would seem to be still in existence, and is thus described in *Archæologia*, vol. xxxi., app., page 475:—"18 April, 1844, Evelyn Philip Shirley, Esq., M.P. for Monaghan Co., exhibited a charter of the 12th cent. [? 11th] from muniments of the Lechmere family. It is a grant of land in Wribbenhall made by Turstinus to the monks of a monastery not specified. The peculiarities of this charter consist, first in its being signed with a cross by each of the persons who made and confirmed the grant; and secondly in the seal being suspended by a thin label, not as usual from the foot of the charter, but from the middle of it. It is believed that this is the only instance

* "Anno MCCXV. Hugo de Mortuo mari fecit fidelitatem de Wrbehale in capitulo Wigornensi de xx solidis annuis, quos antecessores sui ecclesiæ prædictæ contulerant per manus quorundam percipiendos; quibus eo quod redditum suum non redderent et vi ejectis et pretio, ipse prædictam terram suscepit redditum redditurus."—*Annales Monastici*, vol. iv., page 405.

† De Wrubenhale. Quidam homo Thurstinus nomine dedit nobis Wrubenhal: Radulphus de Mortuo-Mari seniore concedente et confirmante; sicut carta ipsius testatur, succedante tempore Rogerus de Mortuo-Mari cepit eam ad feodo firmam. Vnde Priori et conventui fidelitatem juravit, et relevium dedit, et obligavit heredes suos sicut carta ipsius testatur ad faciendum Priori et conventui fidelitatem, et ad dandum relevium pro tempore et ad solvendum singulis annis. In festo S. Martini xx sol. A.D. MCCXL.—*Registrum Prioratus Beatæ Mariæ Wigorniensis.* Camden Soc. p. 20b.

hitherto known of such a singular mode of attaching the seal being practised in England; although something similar exists in the collection of charters in the Hotel de Soubise at Paris."

This same Turstin, who figures here as a benefactor to the Monks of Worcester, was also Lord of Ribbesford; but, as will be seen later on, his character is there drawn by the monks in very different colours.

In the year 1148 Simon Bishop of Worcester in a very solemn manner confirmed to the Prior and Monks of Worcester all their lands and possessions, among which is named Wribenhale. The manor belonged to the office of Cellarer in the Monastery, and was allotted with other places for the particular purpose of buying wood.*

In 1203 Roger de Mortimer did fealty to the church of Worcester of twenty shillings of Wurbenli [Wribbenhall].†

In 1215, as has been shown, Hugh de Mortimer did the like. The following extract relates to Roger Mortimer, his nephew and heir, and would indicate that *the ancient Wribbenhall, or a part of it, became the modern Bewdley*:—"By an inquisition held at Worcester 7 May, 11 Edward III. (1388), before Robert de Longdon, deputy of William de Trossell,‡ the King's escheator for England on this side Trent, it was found that the manor of *Beaulieu* was held of the Priory of Worcester by the yearly rent of 20*s*., which had been paid by Roger Mortimer the elder, Edmund Mortimer his son, Roger the son of Edmund Mortimer, & Edmund the son of Roger & Matilda his wife, who were lords of Beaulieu & paid the rents before mentioned."§

Here the owners of the manor, the persons who held it of them, and the amount of rent paid, are precisely the same as those given in 1215; but the name of the place has been changed from Wrbehale to Beaulieu, or "beautiful place." It was seldom that Norman place-names ousted those of Saxon origin; but the loveliness of the scenery well justified the change in this instance.

---

* Hayley MS.

† *Reg. Prior. Beat. Mariæ Wigorn.*, p. 20b. Cam. Soc. vol. 91.

‡ Sir Wm. Trussell was the judge who condemned the Despencers to death, and pronounced the deposition of Edward II.

§ Hayley MS. This will be more readily understood by reference to the Pedigree of Mortimer in the Appendix.

The earliest mention of the town under its present name appears to be in the Close Roll of Edward I. (1304), when Margaret wife of Edmund de Mortimer is said to have had assigned to her for her better support certain lands in *Beaulieu.* Bewdley was probably a residence—at least an occasional residence—of the Mortimers about this time; for on a mutilated stone coffin lid discovered during the recent restoration of Ribbesford church is a shield bearing their arms:—*Barry of six or and az., an inescutcheon arg.; on a chief gold, gyroned of the same, two pallets of the same.* On the sides are the words, "JE VOUS PRI" and "BON HENRI." Norman-French monumental inscriptions were in general use only for a short time—1290 to 1320; and it is to this period that we should assign the origin of the name Beaulieu or Bewdley. As examples of similar etymology, we find that Beaulieu in Monmouthshire became Bewley,* and Roilieu near Oxford became Rewley. In all the *Inquisitiones post Mortem* of the 14th century it is styled Beaulieu or Beauleu. In the charter of Edward IV. (1472) the name is spelt Beaudeley, showing that the change into its modern form was nearly completed. Leland (1506—1552), who visited the town about 1539, says, "I gather that Beaudley is but a very new town, and that of old tyme there was but some poore hamlett, and that upon the Building of a Bridge there upon Severne, and resort of people unto it, and commodity of the pleasant site, men began to inhabit there; and because that the plott of it seemed fayre to the lookers on it took a French name BEAUDLEY *quasi bellus locus.* I asked a merchant there of the antientnesse of the towne, and he answered mee that it was but a new towne, adding that they had liberties granted by King Edward."

Camden (1551—1623) gives the same derivation. "Bewdley," says he, "takes its name from its most pleasant situation—

"Delicium rerum Bellus Locus undique floret
Fronde coronatus Virianæ tempora sylvæ."

Which Bishop Gibson translates thus—

"Fair seated Bewdley, a delightful town,
Which Wyre's tall oaks with shady branches crown."

* *Taylor's Words and Places,* p. 267.

Dr. Stukeley in a letter dated from Bewdley, Sept. 17, 1712, says, "Were I to choose a country residence for health and pleasure, it would be undoubtedly on the west side of the island, not far from this river (Severn), and where it is most distant from the sea." (*Itin.* i., page 71.)

We have seen that in the time of the Conqueror Bewdley (or Wribbenhall) was given by Turstin, a vassal of Ralph de Mortimer, to the Priory of Worcester. In 1215 the tenant of the Monastery was ejected, but allowed compensation; and then the Mortimers themselves resumed possession subject to a yearly rental of 20*s*. After 1388 no mention of Bewdley is made in connection with the Monastery, and the manor descended through the Mortimers to our own Queen Victoria.

To trace the history of the great family of the Mortimers would fill a volume. It was, moreover, a family so mixed up with the general history of England that the local historian may the more readily pass it over. The founder of the family in England was Ralph de Mortimer, who came over from Normandy with the Conqueror in 1066, and was the King's ablest Lieutenant in the West, and the vanquisher of Edric Sylvaticus, the Saxon Earl of Shrewsbury. As a reward for his services he received the castle of Wigmore, and lands at Cleobury and elsewhere. Again, when in 1074 Roger Earl of Hereford lost his lands by rebellion, they were conferred on Mortimer, who then became one of the greatest barons in the West, and owned 132 manors on the Welsh border. The pedigree of Mortimer (see Appendix) is traced from him.

Roger Mortimer (III.), created Earl of March, married Joan daughter and heiress of Sir Peter de Geneville, and by this marriage the whole inheritance of Geneville and half the lands of Lacy came to the Mortimers. This was the notorious Roger Mortimer, the murderer of Edward II.: he was executed in 1330, and his estates were forfeited. Roger Mortimer (IV.) his grandson regained the patrimony and the Earldom of March. In 6 Edw. III. this Roger gave to John Chamberlain, grandfather of John de la More, custody of all his cattle in his manors of Clebury and Beaulieu and also in the Chace of Wyre.*

* "Rog'us de Mortuo Mari dedit Joh'i Cam'ario Avo Joh'is de la More custodiam om'ium p'cor' suor' in man'iis suis de Clebury et Beaulieu ac eciam chacee de Wyre."—*Inq. post Mortem*, 6 Edw. III., vol. iv., p. 52.

Dying in Burgundy in 1360 he was succeeded by Edmund Mortimer (III.), Earl of March and Ulster, through whose marriage with Philippa daughter of Lionel Duke of Clarence their descendants ultimately succeeded to the Crown.

In 1425 Richard Duke of York inherited the manor, and under his beneficent rule Bewdley made great progress. In 1441 he granted his office of Chief Ranger of his forest of *Were* (Wyre) in County of Salop to Leonard Hastings. In 1446 he obtained a licence for a market every week upon the Wednesday at his manor of *Beaudley*, and for a fair yearly upon the festival of St. Agatha the Virgin (Feb. 5).* Thus in 1446 Bewdley rose from the condition of a village to the dignity of a market town, and in past times the holding of fairs and markets was regarded as a most valuable privilege. The want of a Bridge over the Severn seems to have been then immediately felt, and next year (March 20, 1447) we find the Bishop of Worcester (John Carpenter) in his Castle of Hartilbury granting 40 days' indulgence to all contributing to the building of the bridge lately founded *(noviter fundati)* between the ville of Wrebenall in his diocese and stretching across the Severn to the ville of Bewdley in the diocese of Hereford.

In 1459 Richard Duke of York was attainted, his property forfeited, and £40 per annum from Bewdley was given to Lord Dudley. In the early part of 1460 Bewdley was granted to Edward Prince of Wales, son of Henry VI., to get Wales from the Yorkists; and in December Duke Richard was slain at Wakefield, and his head fixed on York gates with a paper crown on it. Richard's eldest son Edward, though only 19 years of age, was a very successful leader; and within a few months of his father's death he entered London in triumph, and was proclaimed King by the title of Edward IV. (March 3, 1461). It is needless to say that with this change in fortune his father's attainder was reversed, and the ancient patrimony restored. Hence it was that the manor of Bewdley became part of the private property of the Sovereigns of England.

In 1472 Edward IV. granted a Charter of Incorporation to the town, and conferred on it many privileges. (See appendix).

* Cart. 25 & 26 Hy. VI., n. 41.

After the manor of Bewdley became Royal Demesne or Crown Land, it was customary for the King to let it to farm for a term of years, except when it was actually occupied by members of the Royal Family. In the time of Henry VII. Prince Arthur held it and all the ancient Earldom of March in his own hands. In the next reign it was at times the residence of the Princesses Mary and Elizabeth. Some old deeds in the possession of John H. Crane, Esq., show that in 1601 it was leased to Sir Edward Blount. In 1612 it was held by Henry Prince of Wales, and the following survey of the manor was then taken:—

Man'ium de Bewdley — The presentmt of the Jury Sworne at a Court of Survey of the princes highnes of the said manner: as well for the meareing & bounding out of the said Mannor As also for other businesses of the princes highnes to them given in charge there holden the last day of September in the yeares of the reigne of or Soveraigne Lord James by the grace of God of England &c the Tenth & of Scotland the 46th before John Townley Esqr Steward and surveyor of the said Mannor

	Thomas Boylson	Jur'	Ricus Barret	Jur'
	Edrus Hale		Johes Hill de Silton	
	Edrus Tombes		Humfrus Burlton	
	Willus Milton Sen		Ricus Clare	
	Ricus Whitecote		Willus Kaye	
Noia Jur'	ffrancus Dickins	Jur'	Johes Tyler	Jur'
	Walterus Hill		Johes Hardwick	
	Thomas Dedicott		Willus Boylson	
	Johes Hayles		Johes Nash	
	Willus Milton Jun'			

The bounds of the Mannor.

The first meare or bound of the said Mannor or Lordshipp beginning on the sowth side of the Town of Bewley leadeth along by the River of Seaverne unto a meadowe called Blackstone meadowe in the Lordshipp of Ribbesford & so leadeth by the bounds of the said Lordshipp of Ribbesford adjoining to Bewdley parke pale up along to the said parkes end And so to a copice called the Hoockleasowe and from thence leading to another copice called the Hoockwood and from thence to a place called the Rovell parcell of the princes woods & so leading along from Hoockwood hedge vnto a certaine leasowe called porters & then leading by the said leasowe hedge unto a brooke called Gladder brooke, and so over the said brooke unto the lands of Sr Tho:

Conisby knt called parlors and from thence unto certaine grounds heretofore waste and now Inclosed into seu'all parcells in the tenure of divers persons conteyning in the whole by estimacon' about Ten acres, & from thence unto a waste parcell of ground of the Lordshipp of Abbottesley called Gibheath & from thence unto a poole called the Dead poole, and from thence vnto a place called Tybbebach & so to a meadowe called Gavards meadowe & from thence unto the lands of the said Sr Tho: Conningsby & so unto certaine Leasowes called ffoxlies & ffoxlies hill which are adjoining vnto blisse yate & thence leadeth eastward from the Bliss yate unto a Copice of the said Sr Thos: Coningsby called parlors Bynde als-Shutford & so leading to Gladder brooke againe along by a wood called Altonswood unto a place called the Lyehead All which said Lyehead is within the Lordshipp of Bewdley, & so leading by Altonswood vnto a marish ground seggbach And so from the said seggbach leading by Altonswood to Cleobury way And so still leading from the said Altonswood vnto a place called the over end of the Lords yard, And from thence to a place called the Shelfe heald brooke & from thence Down a long by the said brooke so to Dowles brooke & so a long by Dowles brooke, to Goodwater Brooke from the which Goodwater Brooke cometh a great highway, And so by the Lordship of Dowles to Barkehill & so down Barkehill a long by the lordship of Dowles unto the said River of Seaverne on the North side of the Town of Bewdley, & from thence along by the said River of Seaverne to the Sowth side of the said Town of Bewley where the first bound began, And also certain waste grounds of this Lordshipp divers parcells whereof are now Inclosed called Linolls, Hedgewick & good Moore, with the Copices called the old Binde, the new bynde, the new Lodge binde, which Copices are meared & bounded as hereafter followeth That is to say from Dowles brooke up a long by Altonswood unto a Coppice of the aforesaid Sr Tho: Conningsby called Roiose Bynde & so a long Downe by the said Coppice & up againe to Cleobury way, & from thence leading by the said way to Altonswood & so leading along by the said Altonswood to Oledgewick & and from thence along by the said wood to Lempe Brooke & so directly by Lempe brooke to Dowles brooke aforesaid & from thence up to the corner of Altonswood where the last bounds began.

Concerning the Capitall mesuage & the demeasne Item the Jury doe pesent that the prince hath a Capitall mesuage within the said Mannor called Ticknell & a Stable called the Kings Stable togeather with a parke called Bewdley parke, & fair meadows adjoining called the Lady meadowes.

Item they doe pesent that there are groweing within the said parke 3500 old Trees And they value 1000 of them at £1000 And one other 1000 of them at 1000 Marks, & one other 1000 of them at £500 and the 500 residue at 500 Nobles.

The parcke conteineth about 400 Acres (halfe) of it is heath ground wherein by estimac'on there are between one hundred & eighty head of Deere besides the feeding of which Deere the herbage may be esteemed to be worth £xx by the yeare, And the said meadowes called the Lady Meadowes conteine about 34 Acres and are worth £40 by ye year.

Item they pesent that there is no Advowson within this Mannorr but a Chappell, to which King Phillippe & Queen Mary, by theire L'red patents under the greate Seale of England have graunted a Stypend of £viii pr Annu', which is paid by the Kings mats Receivors accordingly.

The Waste and Comond within the Mannorr.	acres	
Item they pesent that the Lodge Copice cont' by estimac'on ..	60	o
Item the parke end Copice cont' by estimac'on	60	o
The new bynde Coppices conteine by estimac'on	26	o
The Coppices called Hitterell Coppices cont' by estimac'on ..	104	o
The old Bynde Coppice cont' by estimac'on	040	o
The Coppices called powcamaston and picamaston conteining by estimac'on 48 acres which are in a lease .... for £xxii p' Annu' & which they conceive to be the worth the rent	048	o
One pcell of waste called great Hedgwick con' by estimac'n ..	240	o
One pcell of waste called ye little Hedgwick, cont' by estm' ..	070	o
One parcell of waste called the Goodmore cont' by estimac'on.	040	o
One parcell of waste called the Lynolls con' by estimac'on....	050	o
The Lords yard, Cold harber & Shelfe head con' by estm'....	100	o

Whereupon are growing about 60 great Trees to the value of £3 a Tree And the vnderwood is worth psently to be felled

One parcell of waste called the Rovell cont' about two acres whereupon there is wood growing worth £3.

	acres	
One pcell of ground called the Lyehead now inclosed cont' by estm'	016	o
The Barkhill conteining by estimac'n	004	o
A waste called Hacidlyes Bind con' by estimation	020	o
The new Lodge Bind conteyning by estimation	024	o

whereupon some wood is groweing worth £6 13*s*. 4*d*.

Intrusions within the Mannorr.

* * * * * * *

The Town of Bewdley.

The Towne of Bewdley scituate within the said Mannorr is scituate adjoining to the said River of Seaverne which Town was Incorporate in the third year of his Maties Reigne by the name of the Bayliffe & Burgesses, The Jurisdicc'on of wch said Corporac'on doth extend to the lymitts of the said Mannorr, Upon the graunting of which said Charter there is reserved xx*s*. p Ann' to the Kings Maties.

Item they pesent that there be four fairies by the yeare & two marketts weekly graunted by Charter, And the roll of ye Marketts and of Bridge are graunted to the Corporac'on by the Kings Matie.

The Bayliff and Burgesses of Bewdley were the next lords farmers of the manor. The Court Rolls commence in 1655, Sept. 4th, Sir Ralph Clare, Knight of the Bath, being the lord, and Adam Hough, gent., steward of the manor. From 1670 to 1673 the Courts were held in the name of Samuel Gardner, gent. In 1673 Bewdley manor was settled in jointure on Queen Catherine of Braganza, wife of Charles II., who then demised the park and manor and first and second vesture on the cutting of Lady Meadows, and liberty to get coals, to Sir Richard Powle, from Michaelmas, 1702 (when Gardner's lease expired), for 40 years, at a rental of £17. 10*s*. 4*d*. She also demised to Sir R. Powle 447 acres of coppice to hold from Lady-day, 1695, for 40 years—rent £17. Five days after this Sir R. Powle sold his interest in these leases, for £1123 and £1081. 1*s*. 8*d*. respectively, to Sir Francis Winnington. In 1674 Sir F. Winnington also purchased for £2765 Gardner's title to the manor for the residue of 31 years. Soon afterwards Charles II. demised a lease to him for 99 years, from the expiration of his former leases. This grant continued the Winnington family in possession of the manor till 1841, when it reverted to the Crown. The Earl of Dudley was afterwards lessee, and in 1870, on the expiration of his term, the whole of the estates (2210 acres), including Winterdyne, Ticknell, Kateshill, Park Lodge, Park Farm, Wharton's Farm, Bowcastle, Uncles', and part of Wyre Forest, together with the manorial rights, were sold to various purchasers.

Tradition relates that the original town of Bewdley was situated on the Wyre Hill at some little distance from the Severn; and an ancient inn—formerly the "Shoulder of Mutton," now the "Old Town-Hall"—had, until recent times, a projecting story with pillars, under which was a covered market. Edward I. granted to Henry de Ribbesford a market on every Wednesday, and a fair on St. Margaret's-day, and this may have been the site on which it was held. It is now quite disused for this purpose, but the houses near it are very old, and the high road went past it till 1753. Such a splendid position on a fine river, and near a forest abounding in oaks, was not overlooked by the inhabitants of Bewdley, and they made use of their opportunities by applying themselves to boat-building and navigation.

In 1412 (13 Henry IV.), in a Parliament held at Westminster, the citizens of Bristowe (Bristol) and Gloucester prayed that they might pass Bewdley without hindrance. "Certain persons of Bewdley having great boats called *trowes* had confederated themselves together for their singular profit, and would let no one pass through the said parts with their goods and chattels, except they would hire the said boats for the carriage of the said goods: & that on the eve of St. Michael last past, lying in wait near Bewdley with great force and arms, they had seized upon a great drag or flote going to Glos'ter (such as complainants had used to make in their parts to carry timber & fuel) & made the masters of it cut in pieces the said flote in the said river, or otherwise they would cut off their heads. They therefore pray free passage, &c." The men of Bewdley do not appear here in a very favourable light; but they seem to have been anxious to protect their own interests, and the place must have been already of some importance.

Leland has left us a descriptive account of the town as it appeared about 1539:—

"From *Kidderminster* to *Beaudly* 2 miles by a fayre downe, but somewhat barren, as the Veyne is thereabout on every syde of *Beaudley* for a littie compasse. I entred into *Beaudley*, in *Schropshire*, as some saye, by a goodly fayre bridge over *Severne* of [five] great Arches of stone, being even then in new reparation.

"This bridge is onely on *Severne* betwixt *Beaudley* and *Worcester* bridge. To this Bridge resort many flatt long vessels to carry up and downe all manner of merchandize to *Beaudley* & above *Beaudley*. The East part of the Bridge at *Beaudley* and the left Ripe of *Severne* be in *Worcestershire*; but many say and hould that the west end of the Bridge and the right ripe of *Severne* within the town of *Beaudly* be in *Schropshire*, & *Wyre* Forrest in *Schropshire* going to the parke of *Tetenhall*. The Towne self of *Beaudley* is sett on the side of an Hill, soe comely, a man cannot wish to see a Towne better. It riseth from *Severne* banke by East upon the hill by west; soe that a man standing upon a Hill *trans pontem* by East may discerne almost every house in the towne, and at the rising of the Sunne from East the whole Towne glittereth (being all of newe Building) as it were of gould.

"There be but 3 Streets memorable in the Towne. One from North to South, all along *Severne* banke. The second is the Markett place, a fayre large thinge and well builded. The third runneth from North to South on the Hill syde, as the first doth in the Valley of *Severne*. The Parish Church standeth a mile lower at *Ripley*,* *ut aqua defluit ripa dextra*. By the distance of the Paroch Church I gather that *Beaudley* is but a very new Towne.

"There was a Privilege of Sanctuary given to this towne that now is abrogated." †

This description applies to the present site of the town, and no mention is made of the old part on the Wyre hill.

Under the Tudors the prosperity of Bewdley was in full tide. Henry VII. enlarged Ticknell House and made it into a Palace for Arthur Prince of Wales, who there resided and held his Court. There, too, he was married to Catherine of Aragon. Henry VIII. granted three charters to the town, and sent his daughters the Princesses Mary and Elizabeth to reside in it. The many distinguished persons who were constantly coming to the town, attended by large retinues, would give increased employment to the inhabitants. To prevent disputes a special law was made to regulate the prices to be charged by the innkeepers (1528):—

"Apud Bewdeley xvi die Nov. a. 19 Henry VIII. For the considerations mentioned in this Bill It is ordered by the Princesse‡ Counsaill that during the abode of the Princesse Counsaill in the Towne of Bewdeley all manner of persons the Princesse Servants or belonging to the said household shall have their horses at Liverie in all Innes and hosteries of the said Town after the rate of i*d*. ob daie and night for hay and litter. And all other Estrangers Sutors and others repairing to the said Towne to pay after the rate of ij*d*. daie and night for hay & litter, &c.

"Henry Collier. Ja. Denton. G. Bromley.
"Thomas Gent. T. Russell. R. Hassall."

Manufactures of various kinds were started in the time of the Tudors, and flourished. The chief of these was cap-making, which at one time afforded employment to probably 1000 people in Bewdley. In the Ribbesford Registers the term "capper" appears as the trade in a large proportion of the entries. Fuller (*Worthies*, p. 49) says that this occupation set no less than 15 callings to work. Machinery was forbidden, and the trade was protected by law. In 22 Edw. IV. a penalty of 40*s*. was inflicted upon any one setting up a fulling-mill. A mill would thicken and full more caps in a day than fourscore

* Ribbesford *in marg*.
† Leland's *Itinerary*, vol. iv., p. 100: Oxford 1744.
‡ The Princess Mary.

men, and it was considered inconvenient to turn so many labouring men to idleness. In 3 Henry VIII. it was enacted that no caps or hats ready wrought should be brought from beyond seas. In 13 Eliz. caps were to be worn by all persons (some of Worship and Quality excepted) on Sabbath and Holy days under penalty of ten groats. This was repealed in 39 Eliz. By an Act of the Common Council of London in 1665 all caps were to be brought to Blackwell Hall except *Monmouth* and *Bewdley* caps. The French Protestant Refugees brought into England the use of hats, and the new fashion caused the decline of the Bewdley manufactures. In the time of Charles II. Mr. Yarrington says, "Cap-making in Bewdley is grown so low that great part of the ancient cap-makers in that town are wholly decayed, and the rest at this present day are in a very low condition." One of the most eminent cappers of Bewdley was Walter Palmer, who lived in High Street, in the house now belonging to Mr. Marcy. His daughter Sarah was married at Ribbesford, Aug. 23. 1688, to Israel Wilkes, grandfather of the notorious John Wilkes, Member for Middlesex, and editor of the *North Briton*. Another daughter married Dr. Jas. Douglas, Physician to Queen Caroline; and his son George married Anne Johnson in 1687, and was grandfather of Mrs. Skey, wife of Jonathan Skey. "Walter Palmer, Bewdley, capper, 1656," and "Thomas Farloe, capper in Bewdley, 1670," issued tokens which passed current in the town for halfpence. The trade appears to have afterwards revived, and to have lingered on till the beginning of the present century. The Worcestershire Guide for 1797 enumerates amongst the callings exercised here "Dutch and sailors caps, which are much prized for their excellent napping." Cap-making is now a thing of the past.

In the time of Elizabeth there were twelve tan-yards in Bewdley, and tanners have been among its greatest benefactors. The neighbouring forests supply abundance of oak bark, and there is no apparent reason why this industry should have fallen off.

In 1697 Mr. Christopher Bancks, of Wigan, started a pewter and brass foundry. This proved very successful, and was carried on by successive members of the family until about . . . years ago, when Messrs. William Stokes and John Smith became the proprietors. It still maintains a high reputation for the excellence of its brass-work. It is said to be one of the oldest manufactories in England.

Among the callings exercised in the time of Elizabeth and James I., as we learn from the Registers, were sherman, carver, glover, trowman, parchment-maker, bargemaker, wire-maker, bowyer, fletcher (maker of arrows), cutler, cooper, walker (fuller), farrier, haberdasher, tailor, collier, joiner, dyer, vintner, carpenter, cardmaker, butcher, baker, mason, fishmonger, glass carrier, staymaker, bedder, clothmaker, saddler, lathmaker, capper, tanner, shoemaker, brickmaker, weaver, fisher, aqua vitæ man, and a salt peter man.

Weavers of sacking and bombazine used to reside on the Wyre Hill. The making of combs, drinking-cups, and other articles of horn has been carried on for more than a century, and now remains as the chief special manufacture of the town.

The market has dwindled by degrees, and instead of 32 butchers holding stalls in the shambles there are now only 2. Formerly the barley market, shambles, and butter cross formed a long range of timber buildings, filling up the middle of Load Street. They were taken down in 1783.

We have seen that as early as 1412 the men of Bewdley had become bold watermen and owned large barges or trows. Latterly a great part of the carrying trade both by land and river came into their hands, and they had the best boats and best crews on the river.* Merchants from Bristol, then the first seaport in the kingdom, established *depots* for their goods in Bewdley and Wribbenhall. Large storehouses were built, and the wares were conveyed by long trains of pack-horses to the inland towns, and returned bringing Manchester, Sheffield, and other goods to be shipped down the Severn to the seaports and West of England. Many old houses here have extensive buildings in the rear, now almost disused. "The number of malt houses," says Nicholls, "in several parts of the town points out another very extensive object of trade, the chief markets for which were some parts of Shropshire, towards Tenbury and Ludlow; but

* Dugdale's "England and Wales Delineated," vol. 1, p. 162.

in later times a turnpike road having been made through those towns to Worcester, the demands from Bewdley were much lessened." Had the Worcestershire and Staffordshire Canal joined the Severn here, as it was once intended it should, Bewdley would no doubt have become a place of great trade. But unfortunately the inhabitants petitioned against the canal, and thus inflicted a blow on their town from which it has never recovered. In 1797 seventeen regular "Trows" went weekly to and from Bristol and Bewdley, and twenty-eight to and from Bristol and Stourport. Thus the larger portion of the carrying trade and commerce was intercepted by the rising little town at the mouth of the Stour.

Before 1801 the population can only be calculated roughly. The number of baptisms from Jan., 1864, to Jan., 1871, was 534, and the population 3021. The number corresponding to this for the 7 years ending Jan., 1602, was 434, and the proportional population would be 2450. At Kidderminster the baptisms for the 7 years ending 1602 amounted to 392, which would betoken a population of 2200. Below is a table of population of Bewdley as given by the census returns:—

1801	3671
1811	3454
1821	3725
1831	3908
1851	3327
1861	2905
1871	3021
1881	3342

The rateable value of the Borough is £8155 12*s.* 6*d.* Number of municipal electors, 501; parliamentary ditto, 1276. Death rate 15 per thousand.

The Chapel.

ELAND relates that a privilege of sanctuary was formerly given to Bewdley; and this statement is confirmed by the preamble to a Bill of Forfeiture against Thomas Crofte passed in the Parliament of 7 Henry VII. (1491). It sets forth that the said Thomas Crofte had "commytted a detestable murder within the Marches of Wales, and thereupon is fledde, and hath taken the Sanctuary of Beaudeley."*

The town of Bewdley was extra-parochial, until by a private Act of Parliament made in the reign of Henry VI. it was put within the parish of Ribbesford. Later still by statute 34 and 35 Henry VIII., c. 26—"An Act for certain ordinances in the King's Majesty's dominion & principalitie of Wales"—it was enacted that Bewdley should form part of Worcestershire, and be within the Hundred of Dodingtre.

As a sanctuary town it would afford a refuge for those escaping from justice; and tradition relates that it was these fugitives who first built the Chapel in the town that they might receive the consolations of religion without going beyond their bounds.

There is also a tradition that the oldest chapel in the town was situated at the foot of the bridge nearly opposite the "Saracen's Head." Dr. Prattinton says that a small building in Ross's S.E. view of the Bridge† was reported to have been

---

* *Rot. Parl.*, 7 Hy. VII., in vol. 6, p. 441a. † See Frontispiece.

Bridge Chapel & Old Houses (pulled down in 1798 to make way for the New Bridge).

the chapel, though in his time it was used as a hearse-house. Mr. Hayley had heard, when a boy, that this building was the oldest in the town; and in the Court Rolls of 1748 this locality was called St. Anne's Corner. Small chapels were often built near Bridges, but Leland's account shows plainly that in his time the chief chapel was situated on its present site at the top of Load Street. "In the towne," he says, "is but a Chapel of Ease, and that is of Timber, in the heart of the towne." The chapel of old was dedicated to *St. Andrew*,* and it contained three chantries, each provided with its own chaplain. The chantry of St. Mary was on the S. side of the chancel and of the same length with it. Its gross annual value in 1545 was £8 3*s*. 4*d*. On the N. side of the chancel were the two other chantries: one of St. Anne—valued at £9 5*s*. 4*d*.—founded by John Washbourn†, and the other of the Holy Trinity—valued at £9 3*s*. 6*d*. In a conveyance of the manor of Dowles in 1544 one part is called "Trynytie Ground, now or late in the occupation of William Weston, Warden of the Guylde of Holly Trinytie in the Churche of Bewdeley." In 1553 the Incumbents of two of the chantries, viz., William Weston and Humphrey Mallet, were living, and received pensions of £6 each from Queen Mary.

Between the two chantries on the north side of the chancel went up a flight of steps from the street into the chancel. A Mrs. Holl told Dr. Prattinton in 1808 that there were houses *under* the chancel.‡ This explains the curious entry in the accounts for 1596 for expenses incurred in mending the "hole out of the Chancell into Mersour Tavarn."§

The chapel was probably built about the time of Henry VI. It was a plain timber structure, and houses were built close up to it nearly all round. Perhaps this accounts for the fact that though it was standing till 1745, no known illustration of it has come down to us.

* Ecton's *Thesaurus* (1742), p. 223; Bacon's *Liber Regis* (1786), p. 379.

† This was probably John Washborne, Lord of Washborne and Stanford, eldest son of Peter Washborne (living 28 Edw. III.) and Isold daughter of Thomas Hanley, of Hanley Castle, heir to his uncle John Washborne (son and heir of Sir Robert Washborne, Kt.) He died at Wichenford 13 May, 1454. His only daughter Isold married John Salwey, and from them are descended the Salweys of Moor Park, the Winningtons of Stanford, and the Ingrams of Ribbesford.

‡ See Accounts. § Ditto, 1596.

Habingdon, who died in 1647, describes the painted glass and inscriptions which were in the chapel in his time. In the east window of the chancel were four panes—in the second, France and England with label of three argent, on each as many torteaux supported with two falcons close arg., the vervels and bells or, having heads of angels covered with Dukes' crowns or. (Arms of Richard Duke of York, father of Edward IV.) On the third, an inescutcheon of four coats—1, York; 2, England within a bordure arg. (Holland Earl of Kent); 3, Mortimer with an inescutcheon arg.; 4, Or, a cross gules (De Burgh Earl of Ulster)—the arms of Duke of York quartering Holland his grandmother, Mortimer his mother, with De Burgh in right of Philippa of Clarence. In fourth pane, Gyronne of twelve argent and gules (Peverell).* In the lower part of the first pane: "ORATE PRO ANIMABUS RICHARDI HERINA"—the rest broken out. In the highest part of the window: "ORA PRO ANIMABUS JOHANNIS GYBBYS, ET ISABELLÆ, ET PRO DOMINO DAVID GYBBYS, RECTORE MATRICIS ECCLESIÆ."† Also: "ORATE PRO BONO WILLIELMI BRADMAKER." In the east window of the north aisle were four panes. In the second were arms of France and England supported with a bull sable horned or and a lion arg. (Arms of Edward IV.: the lion was one of Mortimer's supporters, the bull Clarence's.) In third pane 6 coats blazoning the arms of Elizabeth Queen of Edward IV. In first pane, France and England quarterly label of three, ostrich feathers (Edward Prince of Wales). In fourth pane, France and England, label of three, on each many torteaux, on both sides a falcon arg. beaked and legged or (Richard Duke of York). Under the window was inscribed: "ORATE PRO BONO STATU JOH'IS WIGLOND ET JOHANNÆ UXORIS EJUS QUI HANC FENESTRAM FIERI FECERUNT." In the highest south window of the Lady Chapel were three panes: in the middle one, the Virgin Mary with our Saviour in her arms: in the dexter, a prince with a cap of maintenance and a book under his left arm, subscribed "CRISPINIANE;" in the sinister, a nobleman with a shoemaker's cutting-knife in his right hand, subscribed "CRISPINE." In another window was written: "GLOWCESER CORNESER, RICHAR-

* This coat is still in Ribbesford Church.

† David Gybbes was Rector of Ribbesford 1467—1507.

DUS TAYLOR CORNESER, JOHANNES HAWLL CORNESER." The arms—sable, three goats' heads erased arg. horned or. In another, under some figures kneeling, this inscription: "ORATE PRO BONO STATU JOHANNIS WIGLAND . . . QUI SUNT FUNDATORES HUJUS CAPELLÆ." In another were the figures of three dead persons in their winding-sheets in an erect posture. Over the first: "SUCHE AS YE BIN SO WEARE WEE." Over the second: "AS WEE BIN SHALL YEE BEE." Over the third: "TAKE YEE WHICH OF US THREE." Under a painting in another window: "WILLIAM MONNOX ET ALICE UXOR EJUS, ET JOHANNES BONNER ET ISABELLA UXOR EJUS."

The arms of the Corporation were also in the chapel, and Habingdon describes them thus: "Argent, an anchor az. through a tun or, on the dexter point a sword in chief of the second hilted of the third; on the sinister, a rose gu., with a branch slipped vert."* This description does not agree in some respects with the present Corporation seal and other copies of the arms of the borough as carved on the Bridge, Town Hall, &c. The blazoning of the arms of Bewdley as given by Edmondson is: "Ar., an anchor in pale az., the ring or; the anchor surmounted with a fetterlock of the second; within the fetterlock, on the dexter side of the anchor, a sword erect of the last, hilt and pomel or; on the sinister side of the anchor a rose gu." Edmondson differs from Habingdon chiefly in substituting a "fetterlock" for a "tun." The fetterlock was one of the badges of Edward IV., who granted the charter and arms to the town.

* *Nash*, vol. ii., p. 284.

Previous to the Reformation there were, as has been stated, three endowed chantries, each served by its own priest; and to two of them at least guilds were attached, of which the priests acted as wardens. Guilds were formerly very common in Europe, and were societies of a semi-religious character.* None of the trades assembled to form fraternities without ranging themselves under the banner of some saint. The Guild of "Cornesers, Cordwainers, or Cobelers" † at Bewdley seems to have chosen the Virgin Mary as its patroness, and to have founded the Chantry of St. Mary. SS. Crispin and Crispinian, the patrons of shoemakers, were naturally also honoured with figures in this chantry.

In the reign of Edward VI. guilds were suppressed, under the pretence of their being nurseries of treason and conspiracy, and their property was vested in the Crown. Bewdley chapel was thus deprived of its income, which would probably in these days have amounted to £400 per annum. Queen Mary as a compensation settled a yearly stipend of £8 upon the chaplain, which is still paid out of the revenues of the county of Worcester.

The Chapel Wardens' accounts now come to our help, and from them we gather a few gleanings concerning ecclesiastical matters, commencing at a period of only 12 years after the restoration of Protestantism. The chaplain in 1569 was Sir Thomas Warter, whose whole stipend was £11 per annum and 6*s.* 8*d.* for a house. Clergymen were formerly styled *Sir;* but the title was gradually disused about this period.‡

Mary Queen of Scots, the next in succession to the throne, was a Romanist, and men's minds were still undecided as to which faith would ultimately triumph. In the year in which the accounts commence was the Rebellion of the two Earls in the North, when at Durham cathedral the communion table

* "Gild," says Wright, "is the Saxon for money, and fraternities were called guilds because at first when they associated for charity, religion, or merchandise they cast their money together for the common charge. They had annual feasts at which they chose new officers; and they maintained priests to say mass for the living and the dead of their society. From these sprang the guilds of corporations and cities, and the place in which they assembled was called their guild-hall."

† "Cobbler" was not then a word of contempt.

‡ 1570, "Sir Thomas Warter;" 1574, "Mr. Warter;" 1581, "Thomas Warter, Clerk."

was thrown down and the English Bible torn into pieces. A homily-book against the Rebels was read in Bewdley chapel. The Romish vestments, which had been treasured up for 14 years, were disposed of in 1572, when the collapse of the Rebellion showed that the Reformation was of a really national character. A communion cup was bought in the same year for four guineas: also a napkin for the chalice.

The Bishop of Worcester was at Bewdley in 1572, and Mr. Heward of the *Crown* supplied him with refreshments. The visit next year of the Bishop of Hereford is noticed, because 6*s*. 8*d*. was paid " for wyne and suger to make my Lorde Bishop drinke."

From time to time companies of strolling actors came into the neighbourhood, such as the Queen's Players (1572), the Earl of Leicester's Players (1573), my Lord President's Players (1593); and as there was no other building in the town of sufficient size, they seem to have been permitted to make use of the chapel for their exhibitions! The entry in 1572 runs:—" Paid unto the quenes plaiers in the church—6*s*. 8*d*." It was the custom for companies of comedians to put themselves under the patronage of distinguished persons, whose " servants " they styled themselves; and these visitors to Bewdley seem certainly to have been actors of stage plays, however profane the custom of turning a church into a theatre may seem to us in these days. When Gosson wrote his *School of Abuse* in 1579, dramatic entertainments were usually exhibited on Sundays; and Mr. J. P. Collier's *History of Dramatic Poetry* shows that the Bewdley custom, though rare, was not altogether unknown in England. He says (page 145):—" It is as certain that churches and chapels of monasteries were the earliest theatres as that ecclesiastics were the earliest actors of stage-plays: when the one practice or the other was discontinued we have no distinct evidence. From the following passage in a tract printed in 1572, it appears that even then interludes were occasionally played in churches: the author is speaking of the manner in which the clergy neglect their duties:—' He againe posteth it (the service) over as fast as he can gallop; for either he hath two places to serve, or else there are some games to be played in the afternoon, as lying for the whetstone, heathenishe daunCing for the ring, a beare or a bull to be bayted, or else jack-an-apes to ryde on horseback, or *an enterlude to be played ;* and if no place else can be gotten, *it must be doone in the church.*' "

In 1582 twenty shillings was laid out in "glassing" the chapel. In 1583 comes the first mention of pew-rents, which was 2*s.* 6*d.* for the half-year. Extensive repairs were made to the organ in 1585.

One of the old chantries appears to have been set apart for the use of the Lord President of the Marches and his Council, and the floor of it was well strewn with rushes (1580). The floor of the chapel was only bare earth till 1592, when 4000 tiles were brought from Bristol to pave it.

The Bishops of Hereford and Worcester were at Bewdley together in 1593. A gallon of beer costing 4*d.* was given to the Bishop of the diocese, in addition to the wine and sugar offered to both Bishops. Dr. Lewis was presented with a pottel of wine and sugar and *metheglin.*

In 1594 a new surplice was made from 9½ ells of cloth, at a cost of £1 10*s.* 9*d.* In 1595 five ounces of fringe for the pulpit cloth were bought for 12*s.* 6*d.* In 1596 the bells were rung at the coming to Bewdley of Henry Earl of Pembroke, Lord President of the Marches, accompanied by his wife, sister of the famous Sir Philip Sydney. She was a lady of most cultivated mind, and her influence and popularity in Bewdley are strongly shown. A vacancy occurred in the office of chaplain, and at the Countess's recommendation the Rev. Walter Sweeper was appointed. The townswomen gave a present to her Ladyship of the value of £10 1*s.*, equivalent to certainly £50 of the present money. We are not told what the gift consisted of in 1596, but two years later, on the occasion of a further visit, the townswomen gave her one sugar loaf, two boxes of comfits, and four boxes of marmalade, the total value being £1 10*s.* 7*d.**

* It was to this lady that Sir Philip Sydney's *Arcadia* was dedicated; and when she died, in 1621, Ben Jonson wrote the following lines for her tomb in Salisbury cathedral—

"Underneath this marble herse
Lies the subject of all verse—
Sidney's sister, Pembroke's mother.
Death, ere thou hast slain another,
Wise, and fair, and good as she,
Time shall throw a dart at thee."

In 1600 some mending was done to "stop out the boys in the loft." In 1604 the "waytes" and bell ringing welcomed the entry of Lord Zouche, the new President, into the town. Also a new Prayer-book, containing the results of the Hampton Court Conference, was bought for the chapel. In 1605 a flagon pot of tin was bought, and the church was painted. In 1607 the bells were rung for the first time on "the 5th of November." In 1620 special mention is made of the "women's seats" in the church, showing that the division of the sexes is not a modern innovation. In 1632 long sermons were the fashion, and an hour-glass was set up, so that the preacher might know when to finish his discourse. In 1642 the gunpowder was removed from the chapel into the Court-house! The Civil War was now beginning, and the Chapel Wardens' accounts and Ribbesford registers contain many allusions to the stirring events. Prince Rupert's first entry into Bewdley was in Sept., 1643. The bells were rung; and a hogshead of claret presented to him by the town. In 1644 on Tuesday, June 11, King Charles I. came to Bewdley, and stayed three days at Ticknell. He attended service in Bewdley chapel, and the Bailiff's seat was set apart for his use. The King was in Bewdley again on June 17 and 18, 1645, and slept at the *Angel* Inn.

In 1648 a heated religious controversy arose between John Tombes, minister of Bewdley, and the famous Richard Baxter, of Kidderminster, concerning infant baptism. Wood says, "They frequently disputed face to face, and their followers were like two armies, which led to a breach of the peace, and the civil power was obliged to interfere." Baxter's own account is as follows:—"Mr. John Tombs of Bewdley was reputed the most able and learned Anabaptist in England. We kept fair correspondence for a long time, and I studiously avoided all debates with him about infant baptism; but after a day's dispute at Bewdley my hearers were more settled and the course of his infection stopped. Mr. Tombs and I agreed to meet at the Church in Bewdley on Jan. 7, 1648, where from nine o'clock in the morning till five o'clock at night, before a crowded congregation, we continued our dispute, which was very free in managing our arguments from infants' right of Church membership to their right of baptism." An allusion to this dispute will be found in the accounts, where it appears money was laid out afterwards in mending the seats. Also a quart of sack was given to Mr. Tombes, and a quart to another minister.

In 1650 the triumph of the Rebellion was complete, and tenpence was spent in "putting out" the King's arms. Soon after the departure of Tombes the Baptist, Henry Oasland, a Presbyterian, was appointed minister, and infant baptism was resumed in the church. The annual stipend of £8 was for a few years during the Commonwealth received from the Rectory of Ombersley instead of from the county; and was augmented by the town to £60.

In 1660 came the Restoration, and the King's arms were set up again at a cost of £2 10*s*. A new ring of bells was purchased the same year.

About 1696 Salwey Winnington, Esq., M.P. for Bewdley, built a stone tower to the chapel.

In 1720 a dispute arose between the Corporation and the Rector of Ribbesford about the right of presentation to the chaplaincy. The Corporation repaired the chapel, and paid all expenses; and up to this time had appointed the chaplain.* In stating their case they claimed that the chaplain was really independent of the Rector. "Mr. Hammonds,† however, being a man of letters, life, and parts, by request of many good people in the town, did frequently preach at the chapel; but when he was by Mr. Bailiff Smith and Chaplain Heath locked out, and not permitted to go up into the pulpit to preach, he did not look at this force as any injury done to right: but that some in the town were disaffected to him and unwilling of his labors in the chapel." Counsel's opinion was, that this being a chapel of ease to Ribbesford, the proper patron was the Rector, and the Corporation acknowledged his right under their common seal.

In 1745 it was decided to pull down the chapel and tower and build a new one of stone. The tower was rebuilt at the expense of the Rev. Thomas Knight, Rector of Ribbesford.

* See Chapel Wardens' Accounts 1634, and Corporation Books.

† Rector of Ribbesford 1614—1630.

The new chapel cost about £2200, towards which William Bowles, Esq., M.P., contributed £1300. In response to a brief in aid of the building fund 9517 parishes contributed £607 4*s*. 9*d*., or an average of 1*s*. 3¼*d*. each. The balance was raised by voluntary subscriptions in the town, and the chapel was opened on Lady Day, 1748. There appears to be no record of its consecration; and the dedication has been changed at some time from St. Andrew to St. Anne.

In 1780 the bells were re-cast and the chimes were added. The treble weighs 5 cwt. and the tenor 16 cwt. 2 qrs. 6 lbs. The bells bear the following inscriptions:—

1. When you us Ring we'll sweetly sing
2. Fear God and honour the King
3. Prosperity to this town.
4. Samuel Skey Bailiffe
5. Samuel Kenrick Justice
6. Thomas Rudhall Founder Glocester
7. Nathaniel Adey Bridgewarden
8. Right Honble Lord Westcote High Steward for the Borough of Bewdley.

In 1837 the edifice was repaired at an expense of £1000, and 600 free sittings were added. It was renovated in 1871, and again improved in 1879, when a stained glass window was put in the chancel in memory of the Rev. John Fortescue, the late Vicar. In 1852 a district was assigned to this chapel, which thus became a parish church, but the endowment still consisted only of the £8 granted by Queen Mary, and of about £17 left by Richard Vickriss in 1661. The Incumbent was dependent almost entirely upon the precarious income from pew rents. In 1880, however, Mrs. Fortescue purchased Lower Park House for £2000, and presented it to the Church for a Vicarage. This generosity was met by the Ecclesiastical Commissioners with a grant of £50 per annum. In August, 1882, Mrs. Fortescue by will left a further sum of about £1500 to be invested for the benefit of this church.

Richard Clare, who had a tanyard by Doglane Brook, by will dated May 10, 1618, left 10*s*. yearly for a sermon to be preached annually in the chapel on the first Sunday in the year "to remind people of their mortality."

Incumbents of Bewdley Chapel.

William Weston, Chantry Priest, 1547.
Humphrey Mallett, Chantry Priest, 1547.
Sir Thomas Warter (1569)...*sep.* Aug. 1, 1593.
George Sowthall, 1593—1596.
Walter Sweeper, 1596.
—— Yardley.
Lewis Morris (1605)...*sep.* May 7, 1611.
—— Underhill.
—— Heath, 1615.
—— Wright.
William Madstard.
Manoah Sharrard, 1625—1634.
Robert Morton, 1635—1646.
John Tombes, 1646—1649.
Edward Bury, 1649—1650.
Henry Oasland, 1650—1662.
Thomas Soley, 1663—1669.
Sares Boylston, 1669—1672.
Thomas Boraston...*sep.* July 27, 1706.
John Hassall (1720)...*sep.* 1739.
Thomas Howard, 1731—1778.
William Burrell Hayley, 1778—1780.
Edward Baugh, 1780—1814.
John Cawood, 1814—1852.
John Fortescue, 1852—1879.
William Owen Parker Ford, 1879.

The Bridge.

HE little round boats of wicker-work lined with skins—called coracles—are still in use on the Severn at Bewdley. Another means of crossing the river here in bygone times would be afforded by the Lax* or Salmon ford.†

In 1313 the only bridge between Gloucester and Bridgenorth was at Worcester.‡

In 1447, as has been already stated, the Bishop of Worcester was granting 40 days' indulgence to all contributors to a bridge which had been lately built at Bewdley. William of Worcester, whose collections were made about 1478, describes the bridge in his time as "*de Arboribus*;"§ but the following title of a record in the Tower, cited by Nash (vol. II., app. lxxiv.), would show that in 1460 it was not built entirely of timber:—"*Wigorn' Civitas de omnibus lapidibus pontis de Bewdley et castr' Wigorn' concess' ad reparand' muros.* 38 Hy. VI." Bewdley being a Yorkist town, the stones of the bridge may have been carried off during the

---

* Lax is the Norse word for a salmon. German *Lachs*.

† Nash tells us (vol. I., page lxxxv.) that "many persons in Worcestershire when they bound their children apprentices thought it necessary to insert an article that the master should not feed them with salmon more than twice a week." All search for indentures containing this proviso has hitherto been made in vain, but an entry in the account book of a Mr. Momas, of Stourbridge, shows that formerly this noble fish must have been very cheap and plentiful here. It runs: "24 Nov. 1703 Paid Fosbrooke's daughter Bewdley for a salmon 15lb. 2*s.* 8*d.*" (Prattinton.)

‡ Thomas's *Bishops of Worcester*, p. 160.

§ Nasmyth's edition, 1778, p. 263.

Wars of the Roses to repair the walls of Worcester; and we know that just at this time Bewdley had been seized by the Lancastrians (page 6 *ante*). If the bridge was demolished in 1460, it would have been replaced by the timber structure mentioned by William of Worcester a few years later.

The next notice concerning the bridge is contained in a mandate issued by Richard III.* :—"To our trusty & well-beloved Squier Ric. Croft, know that we have granted the sum of xx marks towards the making of the Brigge of Beaudeley, & have appointed you to pay the same to Walter Res, Wardeyn of the said brigge, &c. Feb. 4 Anno primo (1483)." There is nothing recorded of the building of a bridge here later than this till 1798, so that the bridge erected or repaired in the time of Richard III. would be substantially the same as that which was standing till the end of last century. Leland, whose *Itinerary* was begun about 1538, says:—"I entered into *Beaudley* in *Shropshire* as some say, by a goodly fayre bridge over Severne of [5] great Arches stone, being even *then in new reparation*."

The illustration of the bridge given in this book is taken from a copy of one of the two sketches made by James Ross just before its demolition. The original pictures are preserved in the Council Chamber of the Town-hall.

On the middle pier stood a gate-house of timber, with strong gates on the Wribbenhall side. The north end served as a dwelling-house for the toll-gatherer; and the other was used for a Corporation prison, and was called the Bridge-house.

Two officers were appointed year by year to see that the bridge was kept in proper repair: this office was in existence as early as 1483. Latterly the charge of the chapel, which was Corporation property, was also entrusted to them; and we are fortunate in having a complete set of their accounts extending from 1569 to 1663. Extracts from these accounts are given in the Appendix, and it will be seen that the Chapel-and-Bridge Wardens did not take a very *narrow* view of their functions. Venison-eating, wine-drinking, stage-plays, pillories, whipping-stocks, goomstools, weights and measures, trumpeters, bonfires, bell-ringing, plagues, ship-money, subsidies, excommunications,

* Harl. MSS., No. 433, 1687.

schools, proclamations, conduits, entertainment of distinguished visitors—all these and more seem to have fallen within their province, in addition to their primary functions.

In Nov., 1574, a heavy snowstorm carried away part of Bewdley bridge, and destroyed a great store of salt at Droitwich.

During the Civil Wars Bewdley bridge was an important strategic post. Immediately after the battle of Worcester (Sept. 3, 1651) Major Mercer was sent with a strong party to take possession of it, and on Sept. 4th Cromwell wrote to the Parliament:—"I believe the forces that lay through providence at Bewdley were in a condition to intercept the flying enemy." Mr. William Stokes (now living in Bewdley) was when a boy told by an old woman that her grandfather stood on Stagberry Hill, and heard the hubbub of the battle of Worcester, and saw the Royalists fleeing over Burlish Common. Richard Baxter says:—"Kiderminster being but 11 miles from Worcester the flying army past some of them thro' the town & some by it. I was newly gone to bed, when the noise of the flying horse acquainted us of the overthrow: and a piece of one of Cromwell's troops that guarded Bewdley bridge, having tidings of it, came into our streets, & stood in the open market place, before my door, to surprise those that past by. And so when many hundreds of the flying army came together, when the 30 troopers cried Stand, & fired at them, they either hasted away or cried quarter, not knowing in the dark what number it was that charged. And so, as many were taken there as so few men could lay hold on, and till midnight the bullets flying towards my door & windows, and the sorrowful fugitives hasting by for their lives, did tell me the calamitousness of war."

The bridge appears to have suffered considerably in these rough times, and at a meeting of the Corporation, June 6, 1662, it was determined that "Whereas an Arch of ye bridge is broken down in ye time of ye late warrs, the repaire whereof is likely to require a great charge much beyond what this borough is of itself able to beare, petition is to be made at sessions for assistance from the body of ye County."

The old patch-work bridge managed to hold together till the spring of 1795, when, after a long-continued fall of snow, a sudden thaw raised a heavy flood in the Severn, and the pile that had withstood the floods of more than 300 winters at last gave way. The distinguished Telford was called upon to supply the design for a new structure. In place of five arches he made three—one of 60 feet span and two of 52 feet. He also placed his bridge a little higher up the river, so as to be in a line with Load Street, and this necessitated the pulling down of some houses then standing at the bottom of that street. The work was rapidly completed in 1798, and Telford wrote thus to a friend in December of that year:—"The drought of the summer was unfavourable to our canal working: but it has enabled us to raise Bewdley bridge as if by enchantment. We have thus built a magnificent bridge over the Severn in one season, which is no contemptible work for John Simpson* and your humble servant, amidst so many other great undertakings."

The bridge, which cost altogether £11,000, was opened Sept. 28, 1801. Miles Peter Andrews, then Member for the Borough, gave £3000 towards its erection, and the following gentlemen came forward to advance money on loan:—†

Sam. Baker	£100	H. B. Childe	£250
Joseph Crane	100	Samuel Kendrick	150
J. H. Crane	100	John Brookholding	50
Wm. Slaney	100	Joseph Seager	50
Robt. Pardoe	250	Thos. Compton	250
Jon. Skey	100	J. and W. Cartwright	250
Joseph Child	250	John Phillips	250
W. A. Roberts	250	Thos. Hayley	250
Thos. Crane	250	Wm. Lygon	250
Lord Lyttelton	250	Rev. E. Baugh	50
Hon. E. Foley	250	John Simpson	250
Sir E. Winnington	250	Thomas Telford	250
Wm. Bancks	250	Sir E. Winnington	250
Elizabeth Clarke	100		

Total.. .. .. £5150.

Tolls were charged for passing over the bridge, and the right to collect these was let by the Corporation for £300 per annum. In 1834 the bridge was free from debt, and the tolls were abolished.

* His foreman of masons: buried in St. Chad's church, Shrewsbury.
† Nicholls' *Lecture on Bewdley*.

Ticknell and the Court of the Marches.

N the summit of a hill overlooking Bewdley is Ticknell House. It was formerly a Royal Palace, and many historical associations are connected with it. The name is evidently derived from the Saxon *tican-hill* or Goats' hill ; and this name has clung to it for many ages, though the goats have long since departed. An old poet describes the hill as

"With Mercian Tow'rs adorn'd ;"

but there is no historical evidence to give in support of this statement.

From early times Ticknell formed a manor of itself, distinct from Bewdley, and belonged to the Mortimers.* The manor would imply a manor-house, and we may hazard a conjecture that the Mortimer whose coffin lid is now to be seen in Ribbesford church was the builder, or an early inhabitant, of Ticknell. This would perhaps be the man who about 1290, looking down upon the lovely Severn valley, with the hamlet of Wrbehale nestling at his feet, called it in his own tongue Beau-lieu.

Leland gives us this description of Ticknell as it was in his time :—

"There is a fayre Mannour place by West of the Towne standing in a goodly Parke well wooded, on the very Knappe of an hill that the Towne standeth on. This place is called *Tickenhill.* Whether there was an ancient house in tymes past or noe I am not assured ; but this that now is there is

---

* 3 Hy. VI. *Cal. Inq.* iv., 93. "Tykenhull maner' extenta ampla ; Beaulieu villa ; Sabrin' passag' ultra aqua : Wyre fforest' custod' ejusdem concess' Jo' de la More et hered. Salop.—Edmund de Mortimer, Earl of March."

somewhat new, and as I heard, was in a manner totally erected by K. H. 7th. for Prince Arther. It was repaired for the Lady Marye. Since I heard that Rich. E. of Marche & D. of Yorke builded there. It was Mortimer E. of Marches land."

Ticknell Palace was built largely of timber, and had a great court and garden with several out-buildings, the site altogether occupying two acres. There was a fine park belonging to it containing all the grounds of Ticknell, Kateshill, and Winterdyne within one enclosure. According to a survey made in 1612 there were 3500 large oak trees growing in the park, and 180 head of deer feeding in it. The stable belonging to the house, called the "King's Stable," was situated near Tinker's Gate.* It was a large timber building, often used as a shelter for the homeless (see Registers, 1599, &c.), but burnt down about 1731.

From Rymer's *Fœdera*, vol. xii., 756-762, we get the following description of the marriage of Prince Arthur to Catherine of Aragon :—

"On 19th. May 1499 at 9 o'clock in the morning, after first mass (it being Whitsunday) in the Chapel within the manor of Prince Arthur situated and being near the town of Bewedelay in the diocese of Hereford. The Prince, Roderic Gundesalvi de Puebla, the Spanish orator and proctor to the Lady Catherine, the Rt. Rev. William [Smyth] Bishop of Lincoln, President of the Prince's Council, & John [Arundel] Bishop of Lichfield and Coventry the Prince's Chancellor were assembled by appointment. The proceedings were opened by the Chancellor who (having stated that Dr. Richard Nic had the day before brought a letter from the king, expressing his Majesty's wishes for the marriage, & that Dr. de Puebla was then present with his proctor's commission from the Princess, & that the Pope had given his Dispensation) desired the Prince publickly to declare his mind upon the subject: to whom the Prince replied that he rejoiced at the wishes of his Parents & the Pope, & consented to the marriage taking place, for which he declared himself 'paratissimus.' Dr. de Puebla then declared himself equally 'most ready' to perform the ceremony on behalf of the Princess. The Chancellor then inquired of the Orator if he had sufficient authority, who immediately produced a Proctor's license signed by the Princess herself, with her seal enclosed in a wooden box attached to it by a green silk cord. This license was then read by Dr. Rd. Nic & was to this effect. 'That she was betrothed to the Prince at Woodstock on the 15th. Aug. 1497, that the Pope's dispensation was signed Id. Feb. 1497, & that she appointed Roderic Gundisalvi de Puebla her Proctor generally and specially to perform

* Close to the *Peacock* Inn.

the ceremony in her name, promising faithfully to abide by anything he should think right to do upon the occasion.' This deed was at Majoretum 12 March 1499 signed by the Princess of Wales and the Secretary Michael Perez Dalmacon, Apostolic Notary, in the presence of Gutenius de Cardenas, Head Master of the Order of St. Jacob de Spata, Accomptant General of Castile, Anthonius de Fonseca Major Domo to the Princess Margaret, & Johannes de Velasquez Accompt. General to the Prince. After reading this the Prince put out his right hand, & took hold of the right hand of the Proctor (Richard Poole the Prince's Chamberlain holding both their hands conjoined) and declared that he received the Proctor in the name of the Lady Catherine & the Lady Catherine in her own person, as his true lawful & indubitable wife, promising from that hour so to treat & consider her. Their hands being disjoined, the Proctor went through the same ceremony & declared that he in the name of the Lady Catherine, took Prince Arthur as the true lawful & indubitable husband of the Lady Catherine, & in her name promised so to treat & consider him. The witnesses to this deed are Sir Rd. Poole the Prince's Chamberlain, Henry Vernon the Prince's Treasurer, William Wodhall the Prince's Contra-rotulator, Thomas Poyntz, Dr. Rd. Nic King's Counsellor, Revd Robert the Prince's Almoner, Henry Reynford Clerk of the Council, Bernard Andrew the Prince's Preceptor, Gundisalvus Ferdinandi Rector, Martin Guerrerus, Alphonso of St. John, & Edward Halt. Signed John de Tamayo Apostolic Notary."

The marriage was ratified by King Henry VII. at Calais, May 28th.

After the marriage Prince Arthur continued to reside chiefly at Ticknell and Ludlow Castle; and he was the last Prince of Wales who really exercised any sovereignty over his Principality. Amongst other matters which he was called upon to arrange was a long-standing feud between the towns of Bewdley and Kidderminster. His decision is handed down to us in the following terms:—

"*Ordinac'o'es f'c'e int' ho'i'es & Inh'itantes ville de Bewdeley & Inh'itantes ville de Kiddermyster* 31 Jan. 9 Henry VII. Mem. That it is divised, ordayned, & determyned, att the Cittie of Hereford by the Counsaille of Prince Arthure the first begotten Son of our said Sovereigne Lord, for a finall concord love peace & amytie from hensforth to be had bytwene all th' inh'itants & resiants of the Towne of Bewdeley on the one part & all th' inhitants & resiants of the Towne of Kiddermyster on th' other ptie that they & every one of them shall obey observe fulfill & kepe the Articles hereafter ensuing. In eschuyng all maner gruggs, debats, variances or discords, that now been, or that hereafter might happen to be between them for any old or new matters—First &c. . . item &c. . . . It is by the said Counsell ordeyned & determyned that if hereafter shall happen anie new grugg or variaunce to be betweene the inh'itantes of the said townes, that then they, nor anie of them, take upon them to justify or avenge their said quarrels, but alwaies from tyme to tyme when and as often as the cause shall so require, come & resort unto the said Prynce & his Counsell, ther to show the causes of the same variaunces, & to abide obei & fulfill the direction & determinacioun at all seasons that shal be therein taken by the said Prince & his Counsell.—In witness whereof & of all the p'misses the said Prince hath hereunto putt his signett, the right reverend Father in God the Bishop of Ely, president of his Counsaill with other of the same Counsaill, have subscribed & put to their hands the daie & yeare before rehearsed.

"Jo. Ely R. Powes R. Croft
"Robt. Frost T. Poyntz Newton"*

The following extracts from Churton's *Life of Bishop Smyth* are given as evidence that the Prince did really reside and hold his Court at Bewdley :—

"1500. When he [Bp. Smyth] had proceeded a day's journey on his way to *Lincoln* he was overtaken at Litchfield by express from the King, which obliged him to return to Bewdley, in order to direct certain arduous affairs of the Prince of Wales, who was then at Bewdley, where he had for some time kept his court." †

Again in 1501. "Prince Arthur wrote to the University of Oxford requesting that his servant John Stanley might be elected superior Bedel of the University. Given under our signett at the manor of Beaudley the 12 day of August."‡

After little more than a year of happy wedded life this hopeful Prince died in Ludlow Castle, April 2, 1502.

"The Corps was boielled and well siesed, and conveniently dressed with spices & other sweet stuff. It needed no lead : but was chested, which chest was covered with a good black cloth with a white cross, & sufficient rings of iron to the same.

"The Corpse was removed on St. Mark's day (Ap. 25) from Ludlow to Beaudeley : it was the foulist could windy & rayney day, & the worst way. Yea in some places fayne to take oxen to drawe the chare so ill was the way. And as soon as he was in the Chapell of Beaudley there, and set in the

* Blakeway MSS.
† Page 113.
‡ Page 170.

Quire, therewith such lights as might be for that room the *Dirige* * began. That don the Lords & others went to their Dyner, for it was a fasting day. On the morning the Earl of Surry officiated at the Masse of requiem. A Noble in manner as before [at Ludlow] at which Mass season there was a general Dole of Pens, of two Pens to every poor Man & Woman. From Beaudley Sir Richard Croft & Sir William Overdale, Steward & Controller of the Prince's Horse, rode before to Worcester." †

About twenty years after the death of Prince Arthur, Ticknell Palace was repaired by Henry VIII. as a residence for his daughter, the Princess Mary. The weekly accounts of workmen employed amounted in eighteen weeks to £354 5s. 5½*d.*, and this was at a time when a labourer's wages were about 4½*d.* a day. Amongst the rooms mentioned in the palace are "My Lady's Own Chamber," "My Lord President's Chamber," and "The Prince's Chamber." There is also an account of a payment of 2*s.* 3*d.* for the carriage of twenty-seven loads of bows and arrows, gunpowder, guns, stones, and harness from the manor of Ticknell to the town of Bewdley.

In the early part of the reign of Edward VI. Ticknell appears to have been in possession of Lord Seymour, brother of the Protector Somerset; and it probably came to him on his marriage with Queen Catherine Parr, widow of Henry VIII. The *State Papers* (vol. vi.) contain a deposition made by Edward Rouse concerning certain orders given by Seymour for keeping his house at Bewdley, in Shropshire. When Seymour was executed (March 20, 1549) the manor would revert to the Crown.

After the death of Prince Arthur other eminent men were appointed from time to time to administer justice within the "Marches" ‡ or border-land between England and Wales. The exact limit of their jurisdiction is not very clearly defined; and indeed disputes about it were of common occurrence in olden times. Much curious information concerning the history and

---

* Dirge: from *dirige gressus meos* in Psalm cxvi. 9, which was used in the Office of the Dead.

† From MS. of the time now in College of Arms.

‡ From "Mark," a boundary—a fief held by the tenure of defending it against aggression: whence we get *Mark graf, Margrave, Marquess, Marchese.*

extent of the "Marches of Wales" has been gathered by Sir G. Duckett, Bart., and printed in vol. xii. of the *Archæologia Cambrensis*. We are indebted to him for the following

LIST OF LORDS PRESIDENT OF WALES.

17 E. IV.—The King sent his son Prince Edward to reside there, under the tuition of the Lord Rivers, his uncle; & Joseph Alcock, Bishop of Worcester, was made President.
17 H. 7.—Dr William Smith, Bishop of Lincoln.
4 Hen. 8.—Jeffery Blyth, Bp. of Coventry & Lichfield.
7 Hen. 8.—Jo. Vosy (*Voysey, Voiscie*, or *Vesey*), Bp. of Exeter.
27 Hen. 8.—Roland Lee, Bp. of Coventry and Lichfield.
34 Hen. 8.—Richard Sampson, Bp. of Chester. berland).
2 E. 6.—John Dudley, E. of Warwick (afterwards D. of Northum-
4 E. 6.—William, E. of Pembroke.
1 Mary.—Nicholas Heath, Bp. of Worcester (afterwards Archbishop of York, & Lord Chancellor of England).
3 Mary.—William E. of Pembroke.
6 Mary.—Gilbert Browne (or Bourne), Bp. of Bath & Wells.
1 Eliz.—Sir John Williams, Lord Williams of Thame.
2 Eliz.—Sir Henry Sidney, K.G., and Lord Lieut. of Ireland. He was 24 years Lord President of Wales (during which time John Whitgift, Bp. of Worcester & Abp. of Canterbury, & Henry Earl of Pembroke, son-in-law to Sir H. Sidney, were Vice-Presidents).
28 Eliz.—Henry Earl of Pembroke (1586—1601).
1 James I.—Edward Lord Zouche (1602—6).
4 James I.—Ralph, Lord Eure, Baron of Wilton (1607—16).
14 James I.—Baron Gerard of Gerard's Bromley, Staffs (1616—17).
15 James I.—Earl of Northampton (1617—25—30).
9 Charles I.—John Earl of Bridgewater (1633—39—49).
13 Charles II.—Richard Vaughan, Earl of Carbery (1661—66—71).
24 Charles II.—Henry Somerset, Marquis of Worcester, created Duke of Beaufort (1672—87).
1 W. & M.—Charles Gerard, Earl of Macclesfield (1689), last Lord President.

A reference to this list will explain many of the entries in the Chapel-and-Bridge Wardens' accounts. Ludlow was the town specially fixed for the sitting of the Court in winter time; but the Palace of Ticknell was kept up for the use of the Lords President, and from various sources we learn that the Court must have been held here nearly every summer. One of the reasons assigned for granting the charter of James I. to Bewdley is that it is the "frequent abode and residence of our Council in the Marches of Wales."

On May 6, 1559, Sir Hugh Paulet (father of Sir Amias Paulet, custodian of Mary Queen of Scots) wrote to William Cecil, "I hope to be with the Bishop of Bath at Bewdley before Whitsunday."—*State Papers*, vol ix.

On Jan. 25, 1563, Sir Henry Sydney wrote from Bewdley to Sir Wm. Cecil:—"Sometime since you granted me the wardship of Charles Walcot, son and heir of John Walcot, of Walcot, co. Salop, which I promised to a man of mine. He denied that he was the Queen's or any other person's ward. After much search by myself, friends, & servants, however, I found amongst the Bp of Hereford's records the evidence upon which the jury declared him to be a ward, which I send herewith by my servant Ralph Knight, & which I suppose is recorded in the Court of Wards. I beseech you that such order may now be taken for the possessing & enjoying of him in my name as in like cases is accustomed, and also for some consideration of my great charges in finding him, & of his small living, as the greatest part thereof remains in his mother's hands during her life."—*State Papers*, add. vol. xi.

On July 1, 1586, Henry Townsend wrote to Lord Burghley that "the Council of Wales were agreeable to remove their sittings from Worcester to Bewdley, where all things had been made ready for their reception."—*S.P.*, vol. cxci.

On March 23, 1587, the Earl of Pembroke wrote to Walsyngham from Ticknell that he had sent up James Powell the seminary priest. On the 28th he wrote to the Lord Treasurer Burghley desiring Her Majesty's resolution for the augmentation of the Clerks in the Council of the Marches to the number of 40. He also requested the establishment of the Remembrancer's office, & asked for the reversion of the Examiner's office for Mr. Massinger, Mr. Sherar being then sickly.—*S.P.*, vol. cxcix.

In the *State Papers*, vol. ccxxxii., is a letter from the Queen, dated June 21, to the Earl of Pembroke, announcing that she had directed Rd Shuttleworth, Esq., Justice of Chester, to return to Bewdley to hold the sessions for Wales in consequence of his lordship's indisposition.

"*Apud Beaudley*, x die Julii, 32 Eliz. Appointment of Piers Madoxe, in the room of Roger Gruff *a'ls* Barber as Pursuivant to Lord President & Council."*

"*Apud Beaudley*, 16 Aug., 40 Eliz. Arthur Messenger, gent., was appointed Clerk Examiner in room of Thomas Sherer, gent. (Signed) Pembroke, Rich. Shuttleworth, H. Townshende, Rich. Broughton."*

On April 26, 1606, a grant was made to Sir Robt. Stewart (first High Steward of Bewdley) of the office of Keeper of Bewdley Park and of Ticknell House for life. (*S.P.*, vol. xx.) He retained this concession only till Sept. 20 of the same year, when, for having assigned over the keeping to certain townsmen & thereby caused inconvenience, his patent was revoked.—*S.P.*, vol. xxxviii.

---

* From a large folio MS. book formerly belonging to the Lords Pres.—in 1832 in possession of T. F. Dovaston, Esq., of West Felton, Salop. (Prattinton.)

"1608. Aug. 6. Ludlow Castle. Ralph Lord Eure to the King. Refusal of Ralph Clare keeper of the deer in Tickenhill Park to allow him and the Council of Wales free occupancy of the Lodge for administration of justice in Worcestershire. Requests instructions thereon, & on the patent for the herbage of the park, which is injurious to the deer."—*S.P.*, vol. xxxv.

"1609. July 9. Ralph Lord Eure to Salisbury. Concerning decays of the house & park of Tickenhill; necessity of coppicing the woods."—*S. P.*, vol. xlvii.

"1609. Oct. 23. Ticknell. Lord Eure to do. Is prevented by a pestilential fever from residing at Hereford this winter. Numerous recusants in Monmouthshire. Ministers so scarce that Bp. of Llandaff is obliged to allow laymen to officiate. Project for the support of 6 Ministers to be paid from recusants' fines."—*S.P.*, vol. xlviii.

"1609. Nov. 13. Ticknell. Do. to do. Increase of recusants in diocese of Hereford. Laxity of Justice Williams, who allows them to take the oath of allegiance in modified form. Irregular election of Sir Sam. Sandys as burgess of Worcestershire in place of Sir Wm. Ligon deceased: Sandys being a strong opposer of the jurisdiction of the Council of Wales."—*S.P.*, vol. xlix.

In October, 1615, King James I. was in Bewdley, probably staying at Ticknell. While there he was informed that Sir Thomas Overbury had been poisoned; and though the information pointed at his favourite the Earl of Somerset he ordered a strict inquiry. (*S.P.*, vol. lxxxvi.)

1616, June 19. The King to the Keepers of Bewdley Park. "You are to obey the accompanying instructions, on peril of our indignation and a penalty of £500." [Parchment: Latin.] "Instructions for the preservation of the King's woods drawn up 17 Feb., 1616, and enrolled in the Exchequer. No wood to be taken except for fencing the coppices. The keepers to be limited as to where they take their browse wood, and none to be more than an inch bore, nor heavier than a deer may turn up with his horns. A restraint against the erection of cottages, and the cottagers to enter bonds not to spoil the woods. The keepers to give in their claims into the Exchequer within a year. Swanmote Courts to be revived. Also the farmers of coppices no more to be allowed to shred trees."—*S.P.*, vol. xl.

The necessity of some restraint upon the ravages in the woods is shown by the following:—

"30 Aug. 1623. Complaint of Middlesex to the Pres. & Councill of the waste and spoyle daily committed by the Inhabitants of Bewdley in his Majesty's woods near that town, & particularly one Thomas Smith his wife & daughter being of late taken in the Lords Yarde cutting and carrying away black Poles, & being opposed by one William Fidoe who had charge to loke to that wood, instead of decisting, they beat him very sore and carried away the poles in despight of him, and said they would never cease cutting whilst there was any.—That many of the Magistrates of the town, that should help to right the King against these apparent Wrongs, do trade much in Laths and Clapboards* & such commodities wrought out of these black poles & stolen Wood, & continue the Malefactors in their wrong doing.—urging the President & Councell to take some present course that this insufferable insolence, if proved true according to the information, might be severely punished," &c.

The fees paid to the officers of the Court were as follows :— President £1040, each Counsellor £40, Secretary £13 6*s*. 8*d*., King's Attorney £13 6*s*. 8*d*., Keeper of the House and Park of Bewdley £3 0*s*. 8*d*., Keeper of the Forest of Wyre £5.

Ticknell had been repaired and Bewdley supplied with water by Sir Henry Sidney. In a letter dated Nov. 12, 1576, he says, "I cawsed to be layd out for the making of the conduits of water for Beawdley & Ludlowe & the repair of those two houses, above a thousand pounds."

During the Civil Wars a Royalist garrison was stationed at Bewdley, and strong gates and barriers were set up or strengthened there.† The town was thoroughly loyal, and the inhabitants voluntarily contributed arms and ammunition for the royal cause. A list of those who furnished arms is written on a fly leaf of the accounts.

In Sept., 1642, some forces were sent to Bewdley and Kidderminster to join Lord Wharton's and Sir H. Chomley's regiments. Shortly after this Lord Brookes' regiment was stationed in the town.

Sir Thomas Lyttelton (ancestor of the present Lord Lyttelton) was Governor of the town for the King in 1644, and had his head-quarters at Ticknell. He was, however, surprised by Colonel Fox, commonly called Fox the Tinker, who was Governor of Edgbaston Hall. The tale is told best in Vicars's *God's Ark* (1646, p. 217) :—

"1644. About the 3rd. of this instant May 1644 the active & resolute commander colonell Fox went forth from Tamworth accompanyed with not above 64 men, and that night came to Budeley a very considerable garrison town of the enemies. At his coming to the first court of the guard in the

* Boards cut ready for the making of casks.

† The gates were Bridge-gate, Tinker's-gate, Welch-gate, and Doglane-gate. The two latter were pulled down about 60 years ago.

town, he boldly commanded them, it being in the night, to make way for some of the prince's regiment who desired to quarter in the towne that night, which was immediately granted unto him, both by that and the second guard at the chaines: and so being thus come to the entrance into the towne, his men slew 5 or 6 of the sentinells, & thereby possessed themselves of the towne, & set a guard at divers doors where the commanders, officers, & men of quality lay, all which he tooke with most of their common souldiers, there being about 120 in all. From thence he went to a great Mannour-house not farre from the towne, where he surprised Sir Thos. Littleton a parliament man, and some other gentlemen, took thence 4 brave Flanders mares, and great store of provisions, all which with 40 most gallant horse of the king's cormorants, and as many prisoners, together with Sir Thomas* hee brought into Coventry the very next morning: about which time all the neighbouring cormorants and garrison-souldiers thereabout were raised up in armes with an intent to have rescued their friends thus taken captive & carried away from them, but blessed be God, they came a day after the fair."

On June 11th in the same year Charles I. came to Bewdley from Worcester, and took up his quarters at Ticknell for three nights. His army was with him, and had been pursued from Oxford by Sir William Waller, who was then hastening to Shrewsbury to cut him off. The King called a Council of War at Bewdley June 13th, and as the result of their debate they by swift marches reached Oxford again June 20, and defeated Waller at Copredy Bridge. While at Ticknell the King sent orders to Prince Rupert to relieve York, and this led to the disastrous battle of Marston Moor. He also sent a party of 3000 horse from Bewdley to relieve Dudley Castle, then besieged by the Earl of Denbigh.

In 1645, June 14th, Charles sustained the crushing defeat at Naseby, after which he hastened westwards, and spent the 17th and 18th in Bewdley. Ticknell had suffered so much in the wars that it was not now fit for his reception,† and he slept at the *Angel* Inn in Load Street. He left a garrison in the town when he went on next day to Hereford; but in August the Scotch cavalry fell upon it, and took 70 horse and divers officers. The Ribbesford registers record the burial of several "souldiers" about this time. Hartlebury Castle was now being strongly fortified for the King, and Colonel Sandys

* Sir Thomas Lyttelton was afterwards confined in the Tower of London.

† Dr. Prattinton says that some of the doors of Ticknell, pierced with bullets, were afterwards used as gates for Winterdyne garden.

Old Tickenhill Palace

Whiteman & Bass Photo-Litho London

impressed the neighbourhood to help in the work. The Bridgewardens' accounts show how the Bewdley magistrates enlisted the sympathies of Mr. Turton by a drink of wine, and then "got off our men from going to worke at the Castle."

After the execution of Charles I. the furniture from all the King's Palaces was taken to London and sold. The survey describes "Ticknell Howse with a green court, yard, garden, & offices, & containing by estimation 2 acres, very much out of repair, & valued for the *materials* at £797 4*s*. o*d*." During the Commonwealth the house was left to decay, but some old customs connected with the site were still retained. When Oliver Cromwell died, his son succeeded as quietly as any of the Royal line had done. Bewdley Park was swept, and five halberdiers and a trumpeter gave dignity to the proclamation of the Lord Richard Protector. The stern old Puritans also did not disdain afterwards to drink his Highness's health in wine and beer to the value of £3 16*s*. o*d*. The loyalty of Bewdley, however, was amply vindicated, for at the proclamation of the King a few months later twice this quantity was consumed; and four quarts of sack were given to four ministers that preached. A little idea of the drinking customs of the Puritan magistrates of this time may also be gleaned from an entry in the accounts for 1659, showing that 4*s*. 4*d*. was spent in "Beare Wine & fagotts when that bardgmen weare examined that travelled on the Lord's Day."

After the Restoration Bewdley does not appear to have been any longer a seat of the Court of the Marches, and in 1689 (1 Wm. and Mary) the Court itself was abolished. When Dr. Stukeley visited Bewdley in 1712 part of old Ticknell House was still standing, and we are indebted to him for the original of the sketch here reproduced from the late Mr. Severn Walker's *Antiquities*. Mr. Hayley remembered this portion of the house standing: it formed part of the east side on the brow of the hill, looking towards the town. It consisted of the gate-house, with a dwelling on the south side of it, wherein lived Mr. Edw. Best, and another on the north side which was inhabited by Mr. T. Meysey. Mr. Ingram's house was at right angles to this and on the north side, making the letter L. The first room you

5

come into, or the hall, was said to have been the chapel. In 1624 Charles Compton, grandson of the Earl of Northampton, was baptized in this chapel, and marriages were solemnized there as recently as 1701.

About 1738 most of the old house was pulled down and re-built by Mr. Ingram, who had married Anne Winnington, daughter of Sir Francis Winnington. Some of the inner walls now standing are probably part of the original palace, and about 1880 a lady's shoe of the Tudor period was found in repairing the wainscot.

In 1873 Ticknell House, with the adjoining grounds, was purchased of the Crown by Mr. Joseph Tangye, of Birmingham.

The Corporation.

HE borough of Bewdley was first incorporated in the 12th year of King Edward IV. The original Latin charter is still kept here in an ancient box ornamented with roses. Translated, the charter runs thus :—

"EDWARD by the grace of God King of England and France and Lord of Ireland to all to whom these presents shall come greeting. Know ye that at the humble supplication of our dear lieges the Burgesses and Inhabitants of our town of Bewdley, and on account of certain considerations specially moving us, of our special favour, and certain knowledge, and mere motion, we have conceded, and by these presents do concede, for us and our heirs, as much as in us lies, that our town aforesaid with its precincts may be a free Borough for ever . . . . And that the Burgesses of the said town and their successors should be incorporated by the name of the Burgesses of the Town of Beaudeley and the precincts thereof, And that they should have perpetual succession and a common seal . . . . And that the said Burgesses and their successors should be persons fit and capable in law, And that they and their successors should be able to purchase lands and tenements, rents, services, and reversions . . . . to be held by the said Burgesses and their successors for ever. And of our further grace we have conceded to the said Burgesses and their successors, that each of the aforesaid Burgesses for the time being should be quit through and within the whole of our kingdom of England and our dominion, of toll, bridge-taxes, ferry-payments, tenure between parceners, harbour tolls, tolls for weighing wool, duties paid by ships on anchoring, payments for stalls, service with carts, tolls for weighing goods, payments for feeding swine in a forest, land taxes, payments to the owner of the soil for breaking ground to erect booths, tolls paid for a road through a forest, tolls for repairing town-walls, contributions for making ditches, tolls paid by travellers, tolls paid for unlading goods at a wharf, and of all other customs of and for all their goods and merchandize in all places within our kingdom and dominion aforesaid, as well by land as by sea and fresh water for ever . . . . In testimony whereof we have caused these our letters patent to be made.

"Witnessed by me at Westminster on the 20th day of October in the 12th year of our reign" (1472).

Additional privileges were granted to the borough in the 22d Henry VII., and confirmed by Henry VIII. in 1509 (Feb. 20th) and again in 1525 (Nov. 5th). The latter charter is still in the Corporation chest.

The borough was incorporated anew by King James I. in the third year of his reign (12th Sept., 1606). A translation of this charter is given in Nash's *History of Worcestershire*, where it fills no less than nine double-column folio pages. Except in so far as it has been modified by the Municipal Reform Act, this is still the governing charter of the borough. The right of returning a Member to serve in Parliament was first conferred by this charter; and the ruling body was to consist of a Bailiff and 12 Capital Burgesses.

The Corporation Records contain many evidences of the political struggles of the Stuart times. One of the most unscrupulous devices of the Court party towards the end of the reign of Charles II. was to annul the charters of the country and to grant new ones.

"1684. Agreed that the charter of James I. be surrendered to King Charles II. and that the Bayliffe do attend our Recorder Sir Thos. Walcot and deliver to him our charter and instrument of resignation, who is desired humbly to present the same to his Matie

"PETER BRANCH, Bayliffe. "JOHN BURY, Justice."

The baits held out as an inducement to this surrender were (1) that by the new charter all boats going under the bridge should pay toll to the Corporation; and (2) that they should have power to make themselves into companies, and to keep all strange traders from coming into the town. In case of refusal they were threatened with a *quo warranto*. Before a new charter could be issued Charles II. died, and James II. granted one dated May 4th, 1685.* That charter was held to be good, and

* The original is now in the possession of John Bury, Esq., of Kateshill.

municipal affairs had been entirely regulated by it for twenty years, when it was discovered by some clever lawyer that it was null and void from the beginning; for when the Corporation of Bewdley gave up the charter of James I. they were guilty of an informality. The surrender was made by the "Bailiff, *Recorder*, and Burgesses" instead of the "Bailiff and Burgesses." This being the case, the old charter of James I. was still in force. But then it was found that only one old burgess, Samuel Slade, was alive; and he alone could do no legal act whatsoever by virtue of it, since by that charter the *major part* of the Corporation was made necessary to such legal act. Queen Anne consequently in 1708 granted a new charter, restoring and confirming the charter of James I., and nominating persons to fill its offices. The Herbert and Winnington families were then contending keenly for supremacy in the borough, and many lawsuits resulted. For two years, in consequence of the two charters, Bewdley had two Corporations and two Bailiffs, who fulminated against each other like rival Popes.

"12 May 1708 Whereas Sam. Slade Tanner hath for ten dayes last past presumed to take upon him the office of Bayliffe of this Borough, &c. . . . . and whereas, &c. . . . . we declare the proceedings of the said Sam. Slade null & void."

Salwey Winnington was elected Member of Parliament under one charter, and Slade's party elected Henry Herbert of Ribbesford. On the case being brought before the House of Commons, it was decided by 211 to 132 that Slade was the rightful bailiff, and so Herbert was returned. Before the next election, two years later, an immense change had come over the feeling of the country, and a Tory majority was in Parliament. One of the first uses made by it was to carry a motion "That the Charter dated April 20th, 1708, attempted to be imposed on the Borough of Bewdley, against the consent of the ancient Corporation, is void, illegal, and destructive to the constitution of Parliament." Steps were taken to repeal the charter, and it only escaped annulling by the death of Queen Anne in 1714; and that day was observed by members of the Corporation for many years as a day of rejoicing for its preservation. This charter has not since been disputed, and the original is still in the possession of the Corporation.

There are very clear indications in the Corporation books of the means employed by Charles II. and James II. to pack Parliament in the attempt to overthrow the Church of England and the liberties of the country. In the new charters the power had been reserved to the Crown of dismissing magistrates at pleasure; and a committee of seven persons, including the infamous Judge Jeffreys, sat at Whitehall to regulate municipal elections. Local committees all over the country corresponded with this central board; and as Parliamentary elections were then exclusively in the hands of the Corporations, the influence exerted would be immense. Here is a specimen of their work:—

"Sept. 12, 1688. 4 James II. In obedience to an order of his Majty's Privy Council Tho: Watmore, Tho: Burlton & Sam. Sandys Esq. 3 Burg. & Henry Townshend Esqre Chief Recorder were all of them voted & removed out of their sd several places And in obedience to his Majty's Lrs of Recommendation to us directed John Bury Humfry Yarranton & Higgins James Esqre were elected & chosen Burg. instead of Watmore, &c., and John Soley Esq. elected Recorder in stead of Townshend,"

The King's tyranny soon bore its natural fruits, and when the expedition of William of Orange was on its way for the defence of the English liberties and religion, James hastily issued a proclamation promising to restore the ancient charters. On the 27th of October, 1688, it was agreed at Bewdley "that his Majesty's most gracious offer be thankfully accepted." But James's offer was too late. Within a week William landed in Torbay, and found the whole country on his side. On Jan. 6th following, the Prince of Orange's letter to the Bayliff of Bewdley summoning a *free* Parliament was delivered, and a verbatim copy of it is entered in the Corporation Books. On the 11th Henry Herbert was elected to the "Convention" Parliament, which placed William III. on the English throne.

In 1668 the Corporation started a small mint of their own, and issued the "Warden's half-peny of Bewdley" to the value of £30. It is an octagonal piece of brass stamped with the borough arms. The Bridgewardens were required to exchange these tokens, when called upon, for current silver.

A list of the Members for Bewdley is given in the Appendix. Before the Reform Act of 1832, which enlarged the constituency and added Stourport to the parliamentary borough, the Corporation was almost always under the influence of some nobleman or gentleman owning property in the neighbourhood. Such were the Clares, Herberts, Foleys, Lytteltons, and Winningtons. The Corporation, however, were not guided solely by their agreement with the political views of their Members. For a long period considerable sums of money were paid as the price of the seat—usually £2000 to £3000 after each election. In 1819, when W. Aylesbury Roberts, Esq., who lived in the town and spent a large fortune there, was returned, this practice was discontinued. This old custom provided for many useful improvements being made in the town; and the Corporation still possess £3000 derived from this source.

There have been many keenly contested elections in Bewdley, and much consequent litigation. One memorable instance was in 1768, when the candidates were the Hon. Thomas Lyttelton (afterwards the "wicked" Lord Lyttelton) and Sir E. Winnington. A quarrel had arisen between Adam and James Prattinton and Sir E. Winnington about some meadows; so the Prattintons went over to the enemy and elected 10 new Burgesses to turn the scale. Some Act, requiring Burgesses to be elected at least 12 months before they could vote for a Member, gave the victory then to Sir Edward; but in five succeeding Parliaments the Lyttelton interest prevailed.

The Municipal Reform Act of 1835 changed the title of the chief magistrate from Bailiff to Mayor. Slade Baker, Esq., of Sandbourne, was the last Bailiff and the first Mayor of Bewdley, and he is the only survivor of the old close Corporation. Lists of Bailiffs, Mayors, High Stewards, Recorders, and Deputy Recorders of Bewdley are given in the Appendix.

Nonconformist Chapels and Meeting Houses.

THE oldest Dissenting community in Bewdley is that of the Baptists, and its origin is said to be unique. In 1646 John Tombes, B.D., a man of great ability and a native of Bewdley, was appointed Curate of St. Anne's. He entertained very strong objections to infant baptism, and so, while still retaining his office in the Church, he founded a separate Baptist society, which numbered 20 persons. George Fox tells us that "Tombes said he had a wife, and he had a concubine; and his wife was the baptized people (Baptists) and his concubine was the world (Churchmen, Presbyterians, Quakers, and all other non-Baptist parishioners)." In his *Apology for the Two Treatises on Infant Baptism*, 1646, 4to, page 66, printed while he was at Bewdley, Tombes says that he "must needs say the Churches that have no other than Infant Baptism are no true Churches nor their Members Church Members." He disputed with Richard Baxter at Bewdley, Jan. 1, 1649, and afterwards held three other public disputes at Ross, Abergavenny, and Hereford. In 1650 he removed to Leominster, when he was succeeded at St. Anne's by Edward Bury, and in his Baptist ministry by John Eccles. Mr. Eccles commenced preaching at Bromsgrove also; and formed the Baptist church there which still exists.* Bewdley and Bromsgrove continued united down to 1670. The following is an incomplete list of the various

* The Cannon Street chapel in Birmingham was in turn an off-shoot from Bromsgrove (1737).

ministers of Bewdley Baptist Chapel since the days of Mr. Tombes:—John Eccles, — Clark, — Thompson (who declined into Socinianism and was deprived 1718), James Kettilby (1718-1767), John Blackshaw (1774-1779), John Pyne (1781-1788), — Baylis, George Williams (1793-1799), George Brookes (1802-1844) and Thomas Griffin (1802-1808) co-pastors*, W. E. White (1843-1846), G. Cozens (1846-1854), J. Bailey (1855-1857), George James (1857). The chapel was erected in 1764.

It is a curious coincidence that the Presbyterian following in Bewdley, which in age ranks next to the Baptists, should also have been founded by a minister of St. Anne's in the time of the Commonwealth. Henry Oasland was appointed within a few months of the departure of John Tombes, and held office until the Act of Uniformity was passed in 1662, when for conscientious scruples which we cannot but respect he seceded from the Church. From the Corporation books we find that several of the burgesses of Bewdley refused to declare against the "Solemn League and Covenant" in the time of Charles II.; and these no doubt were of those who adhered to their old teacher and welcomed his son Edward as their pastor. The Presbyterian chapel here is said to have been built about 1680, and for many years it had a large and influential congregation. In common with nearly all the Presbyterian meeting-houses—400 in number—founded about that time, it has since lapsed into Unitarianism, and has now very few adherents in the town.

Jabez Reynolds by will dated 27th Feb., 1710, left 10*s.* each yearly to the Rector of Ribbesford and the Preacher at the Meeting-house to buy Bibles or religious books for poor children. For his trouble each minister was to have *a bottle of Sack.*

James Clark by will dated 24th May, 1765, left £500 to be put out to interest—one-fifth to be paid to the minister of the Presbyterian meeting-house, and four-fifths among poor people residing in Bewdley. In addition he ordered that the rest of his personal estate after payment of debts, &c., should be given to the poor of Bewdley. The total Consols now is about £1300, and the charity is administered by special trustees.

* In 1808 Mr. Griffin went to Kidderminster, and Mr. Brookes remained sole pastor till his death in 1844. He left £2000 as an endowment for the Bewdley minister, and also 700 volumes for his library.

In the chapel is a marble monument with Latin inscription, thus translated by Dr. Prattinton (probably the donor):—

"To perpetuate the remembrance of Samuel Kenrick this tablet was erected by P. P. Literature was his delight, of manners gentle, of the Supreme Being a devout worshipper, In integrity of life a bright example. He died Oct. 6, 1811, aged 83."

The site on which the Friends' meeting-house now stands was purchased for the Society in 1691, and the building was probably erected soon afterwards. The Registers are at Somerset House (No. 666). Births 1683 to 1767; marriages 1679 to 1758; burials 1682 to 1838. In the small burial ground attached to this quiet little chapel, Mary Darby wife of the *first* Abraham Darby was buried in 1718. There are also stones to the memory of the Cotterell, Zachary, and Sturge families.

In March, 1779, the Rev. John Wesley preached at Bewdley, in an open space in Load Street, to a very numerous and quiet congregation. He was at Bewdley again in 1781, and preached as before in the open air. At the commencement of the service a man began beating a drum, but was soon silenced by a gentleman of the town. Five years afterwards Wesley visited Bewdley once more, and then recorded in his journal, "Prejudice is now vanished away. The life of Mr. Clark turned the tide, and much more his glorious death." From Bewdley he went on to Stourport, "a small well-built village," where he speaks of Mr. Heath, "a middle-aged clergyman and his wife and two daughters, whose tempers and manners, so winning soft, so amiably mild, will do him honour wherever they come." In 1790 he was again at Stourport, "which was twice as large as two years ago. They seemed to be serious and attentive while I was speaking, but the moment I ceased, fourscore or a hundred of them began talking all at once. I do not remember ever to have been present at such a scene before. This must be amended, otherwise (if I should live) I will see Stourport no more." He died March, 1791, aged 88.

The Wesleyan chapel in Bewdley was opened for divine service in 1795 by Dr. Cooke, a clergyman of the Church of England. The head-quarters of the circuit are at Stourport.

The Grammar School, Charities, &c.

THE earliest school in Bewdley seems to have been taught by the curate in some room adjoining the chapel. In 1577 the sum of 2s. 8*d*. was spent by the Wardens "to put the scholemaster's chambers in order." William Monnox, of Bewdley, tanner, by will dated 17th Feb., 1591, left £6 per annum for a Grammar School, payable out of the Pentrenant estate in Montgomeryshire. Gregory, John, and Thomas Ballard by deed in 1599 gave the land whereon the old Grammar School was built. Humphrey Hill, of Silvington, also in 1599, left several houses and other property for the same purpose; and the present school and school-house are built on part of it. King James I. in his charter of 1606 re-founded the school "for the better education of young children and youths, in good arts, learning, virtue and instruction, always to be brought up and informed, which shall be called the 'Free Grammar School of King James in Bewdley,' wherein shall be one master and one usher."

Other benefactors were Thomas Weaver, 1609; John Millward, 1610; Richard Clare, 1618; Mr. Barber, 1619; John Clare, 1621; Hugh Pooler, 1621; William Keye, 1625; John Tyler, 1626; Joan Tyler, John Wakeman, 1640; John Lowe, 1643; Richard Vickaris, 1661; Thomas Cooke, 1693; and John Carruthers Crane. The Rev. Thomas Wigan (1819) gave to the Rector of Ribbesford and the Master of the Grammar School his library of about 1500 volumes in trust for the clergy and other respectable inhabitants of the town and neighbourhood.

Several of the gifts have since been lost. About 1750 the Corporation, who were then the Governors, let most of the school property on lease for 500 years at low rentals. In 1835 the Court of Chancery intervened and annulled the long leases; but kept the school closed for 30 years. Mainly by the exertions of Mr. R. H. Whitcombe, a fresh scheme was obtained, and the new school-room in High Street was built in 1865. In 1882 a further scheme for the management of the foundation was drawn up by the Endowed School Commissioners, under which the government is vested in the High Steward, the Mayor, five Representative Governors, and five Co-optative Governors.

Many men who have attained eminence in Church and State have been educated at this school. Among these were Richard Willis, Bishop of Winchester; Edward Feild, Bishop of Newfoundland; John Medley, Bishop of Fredericton; John Tombes, Master of the Temple and one of the "Triers;" Canon Hugh Stowell; Rev. John Venn, of Hereford; Dr. John Beddoe, F.R.S., President of the Anthropological Society; Rev. J. G. Breay, of Birmingham, &c.

List of Head Masters of the Grammar School.

Manoah Sharrard	1625—1634
John Graile	1635 ......
George Lowe	 1663
James Spilsbury	1664 ......
Nathaniel Williams	 1701
John Cupper	1701—1720
Butler Cowper	1720—1732
Thomas Howard	1732—1778
William Morgan	1778—1805
John Cawood	1805—1835
William Grist...	1866—1871
John Richard Burton	1872

The Bewdley Charity Schools were founded in 1785, and the National Schools in 1830. A Home Mission, conducted by Miss Pountney, led to the erection in 1869 of the school and mission-room on the Wyre Hill.

The Bewdley Institute was opened in 1877. Mr. Edward Pease bought the old "Wheat Sheaf" Inn and other property, which he generously gave as the site, besides subscribing £500 to the building fund. £1000 was also raised by voluntary contributions in the town and neighbourhood. Lord Lyttelton was elected its first president, and Mr. John Gabb the first chairman. With this Institute are amalgamated the old "Literary Society" and the "Working Men's Institution."

The space at our disposal does not allow of a detailed account of the many charities of Bewdley, but it is fitting that we should record the names and mention the gifts of the

BENEFACTORS.

Sir John Hibbots (1595).—Two mills for the poor.

John Millward (1610).—Rent-charge for poor.

Sir William Seabright (1620).—Loaves for poor.

Samuel Sayers (1625).—Six Almshouses in the Lower Park.

Humphrey Burlton (1645).—Nine Almshouses in Park Lane

Francis Gilding (about 1650).—Land for the poor.

Richard Vicaris (1661).—School, Chapel, and poor women.

Sir Henry Herbert (1673).—Bread for poor.

Thomas Cooke (1693).—Eight Almshouses in High Street.

John Hammonds (1714).—£150 to poor.

Ralph Smith (1732).—£50 to Charity School.

William Crump (1754).—£200 for poor widows.

James Clark (1765).—£500 to Presbyterian minister and poor.

John Hurst (1808).—£10 for bread.

Wilson Aylesbury Roberts (1813).—£200 for ten poor widows.

Caroline Aylesbury Roberts (1827).—£216 13*s*. 4*d*. for ten poor women.

Ellen Vobe (1840).—£500 for twelve old maids.

Ellen Vobe (1840).—£100 to Sayers' almsmen.

Mary Watkins (1842).—£100 to Sayers' almsmen.

Mary Watkins (1842).—£250 for Burlton's almspeople.

Rev. Joseph Crane (1860).—£200 for repair of Cooke's Almshouses.

James Tart (1875).—£100 for repair of Cooke's Almshouses.

James Fryer (1856).—£2000 to Bewdley National School.

Mary Blackford (1873).—£2200 in Consols for coal, blankets, and clothing.

William Essington Essington (1878).—£100 for poor.

John Sherriffe.—Land for apprenticing boys.

Mrs. Marlowe.—6*s*. 11*d*. per annum to poor attending Baptist Chapel.

Illustrious Men.

EFORE this history is brought to a close some mention must be made of the various public characters who have in any way been connected with the town. The Royal personages and the Lords President of the Marches of Wales, who so often resided at Bewdley, have already been mentioned at some length.

Sir CHARLES COMPTON, son of Spencer Lord Compton* and grandson of William Earl of Northampton, was probably born at Ticknell, and was baptized in the old chapel there on Nov. 25th, 1624. He fought with distinction in the battles of Edge-hill and Hopton Heath, and is said to have been eminent for "sobriety, moderation, conduct, vigilance, and activity." His chief exploit was the taking of Beeston Castle in Cheshire, when, with only six men disguised as butchers and bakers, he surprised the astonished garrison in their beds. After the Restoration he was advanced by the King to a position of trust, but a fall from his horse at Northampton caused his death in the prime of manhood.

JOHN TOMBES was born at Bewdley in 1603, and educated at the Grammar School. At the early age of 15 he entered at Magdalen Hall, Oxford, and after a brilliant college career was chosen public catechetical lecturer, though being then only 21

---

* Ancestor of Lord Alwyne Compton, Dean of Worcester, and Prolocutor of Convocation.

years of age. He was afterwards presented to the Vicarage of Leominster. When the Civil War broke out he fled to Bristol, and General Fiennes, who had then the command of that city, gave him the living of All Saints there. After the taking of Bristol by the Royalists Tombes escaped to London, where he was soon appointed minister of Fenchurch. Here he utterly refused to allow the baptism of infants in his church, and in consequence was deprived of his stipend. Promising not to introduce this controversy into the pulpit, he was chosen preacher of the Temple, and held this important office for four years. He was dismissed from the Temple for publishing his first treatise on Infant Baptism; and he then returned to his native place, and was chosen minister of St. Anne's, Bewdley. His love of argument followed him here, and, as we have seen, he formed a separate society of those of his own way of thinking. On New Year's-day, 1649, he had the famous dispute with Richard Baxter in Bewdley chapel, when many members of the Universities are said to have been present. He was next presented to the parsonage of Ross; and this he resigned upon having the Mastership of the Hospital at Ledbury. His opinions about baptism alienated his people, and he removed again to Leominster. In 1653 he was appointed to be one of the "Triers" of ministers, which is a proof that his character and learning were held in high esteem. After the Restoration he married a rich widow, and went to reside at Salisbury, where he conformed to the Church as a lay-communicant, but would not again accept any benefice. He died at Salisbury May 25, 1676, aged 73.

HENRY OASLAND was born in the parish of Rock, and after spending some years at the Bewdley Grammar School under Mr. John Graile, he entered at Trinity College, Cambridge. His religious experiences have come down to us in a quaint MS. autobiography which has been printed in the Bewdley *Parish Magazine*. Within a few months after the departure of John Tombes from Bewdley, Mr. Oasland was chosen minister of the chapel, where he preached zealously for twelve years. His views on Infant Baptism were directly opposed to those of Tombes, and he was a great friend and companion of Richard Baxter, with whom he frequently went to preach the "double lecture" in the country. Baxter describes him as having "a strong body, a zealous spirit, and an earnest utterance." In 1660 he married Miss Maxwell of Bewdley. In 1661 he was imprisoned by Sir John Pakington on the evidence of a forged letter, which seemed to imply that he was plotting against Sir Ralph Clare. In 1662, on his refusal to comply with the Act of Uniformity, he was deprived of his benefice. He died in 1703, aged 80 years, leaving two sons, of whom the elder, Edward, was Presbyterian minister at Bewdley many years. Henry Oasland's printed works were *The Dead Pastor yet Speaking* and *The Christian's Daily Walk.*

JOHN BORASTON was Rector of Ribbesford from 1630 to 1688. He was an ardent Royalist, and it is rather surprising that he was permitted to retain his benefice throughout the Commonwealth. An attempt was made to deprive him of it, and among his offences enumerated were—

"That the said Boraston did officiate second servise at the alter, so called, in the chapell of Bewdley, with his surplus and hood in June 1644, or thereabouts,* notwithstandinge an ordinance of Parliament to the contrary."

"That the said Boraston gave warninge to his parishioners of Ribsford to observe the 25th day of December 1648 commonly called Christmas Day. And havinge assembled some of the parishioners preached unto them on the said day, in the said churche, and exhorted them to the observance thereof, notwithstandinge an ordinance of Parliament to the contrary."

"That the said Boraston did voluntarily lende severall sumes of money to the King's Commissioners at Woster against the Parliament. That he went to the King's Courte in Glostershire, and to the King's army lyeing before Gloster, and held intelligence with the Lord Viscount Falkland, then Secretary to his Majesty."

"That the said Boraston is of a very proud and contentious spiritt, and doth lord it over his parishioners, callinge honest men knaves and honest women witches."

In 1673 Mr. Boraston was made Prebendary of Moreton Magna in Hereford Cathedral, and in 1688 he died at the ripe age of 85. One of his sons, George Boraston, M.A., of Wadham College, Oxford, was the author of *The Royal Law, or the Golden Law of Justice and Charity*, and of a *Sermon preached at the anniversary meeting of the gentlemen inhabitants of London, and others born*

* This was probably on the occasion of King Charles' visit to Bewdley.

within the County of Worcester—29th Nov., 1683." Another son, Thomas Boraston, M.A., was chaplain of St. Anne's, and succeeded his father as Prebendary of Moreton Magna.

George Hopkins, M.A., was born at Bewdley April 25, 1620, and was son of William Hopkins, a man of importance in the town, and a great friend of Richard Baxter (see Ribbesford Registers 1609, Oct. 30, and 1647, July 21). He was educated at the Grammar School, and after taking his degree at Oxford was appointed minister of Evesham. "He was very judicious, godly, moderate, peaceable, and upright," and wrote *Salvation from Sin.* (Wood's *Athen. Oxon.)* Dr. William Hopkins, the learned Prebendary of Worcester, and friend of Dean Hickes and Lord Somers, was a son of the above. *(Nash,* supplement, page 1.)

John Inett was born at Bewdley, and educated at University College, Oxford (M.A. 1669). He was appointed "Chauntor of Lincoln Cathedral and Residentiary thereof" 1681. He wrote a valuable *History of the English Church*, 2 vols., 1704 and 1710.

Richard Willis was the son of William Willis, a tanner in Bewdley, and was born Jan. 17, 1664. His mother's maiden name was Susanna Inett, and it is very probable that she was a sister of the above-mentioned Rev. John Inett. Richard was educated at the Grammar School under Nathaniel Williams, Rector of Dowles, and the Master was so proud of his scholar's abilities that he persuaded the Rev. William Hayley (an ancestor of Mr. Bury, of Kateshill) to send him to Oxford. Mr. Hayley, who was afterwards Dean of Chichester, was then a Fellow of All Souls, and so Willis entered at this college, of which by and bye he himself became a Fellow. As Lecturer of St. Clement's in the Strand he became remarkable for *extempore* preaching, and was recommended to King William III. as a proper person to accompany him to Holland: this led to his appointment as Chaplain-General of the Army. In 1695 he was made Prebendary of Westminster, and in July, 1698, was appointed Sub-Preceptor to the young Duke of Gloucester, heir to the throne. In 1700 Dr. Willis was made Dean of Lincoln, and soon afterwards preached the first sermon delivered on behalf of the Society for the Propagation of the

Gospel. In November, 1714, Dr. Willis was nominated Bishop of Gloucester; in 1721 he was translated to Salisbury; and in 1723 he was further promoted to Winchester, which latter promotion he is said to have gained by his vigorous speech against Atterbury. After holding the see of Winchester eleven years, Bishop Willis died Aug. 10, 1734, at Chelsea, aged 71 years, and was buried in Winchester cathedral, where a magnificent marble monument with recumbent effigy of him may be seen.

Alderman Best, who lived in part of Ticknell, was fond of painting and had a museum. He published the *Prospect of a Poem on humane Life and Depravity (with an Episode on the Christian Religion), Death, Judgment, Heaven, and Hell*, in 2 parts, 1735: London.

Peter Prattinton was the only son of William Prattinton, of Bewdley, and was born in 1776. He was educated at Christ Church, Oxford, where he took the degree of M.B. Being possessed of private means, he gave up the practice of medicine, and devoted himself with indefatigable assiduity to antiquarian pursuits. His researches were chiefly made to elucidate the history of his native county, and his MS. collections for *Worcestershire*, which fill many volumes, were bequeathed to the Society of Antiquaries, by whom they are carefully preserved. The roll of "Household Expenses" of Bishop Swinfield (1289) was discovered by Dr. Prattinton among the muniments of Sir T. Winnington at Stanford Court, and it was published in 1853. He died July 11, 1845, aged 69, and was buried at Ribbesford.

John Cawood was born at Matlock in 1775, and graduated at Oxford in 1801. He was ordained in 1800 to the Curacy of Ribbesford and Dowles, of which he had the sole charge. He formed at Bewdley what was probably the first Sunday School in the county, and also began a mission in the Far Forest, which ultimately led to the erection of the new church there. In 1805 he was appointed Master of the Grammar School, and was most successful in his scholastic work. Many of his pupils afterwards attained positions of eminence and usefulness. Among them were Bishop Field, Bishop Medley, and Hugh Stowell. In 1814 he was appointed minister of St. Anne's, and his earnest discourses there during a period of forty years exerted an immense influence in Bewdley. The local branch of the Church Missionary Society, founded by him in 1816, has contributed upwards of £6000 to the good work. He died Nov. 7, 1852, and was buried at Dowles. His published [illegible] and two volumes of *Sermons*.

[illegible] physician and philanthropist [illegible] Feb. 27, 1856, aged 87, and bequeathed £2000 to the Bewdley National Schools, £4000 to the Worcester Infirmary, £900 for the Forest church, besides substantial sums to the Worcester Museum and other useful objects.

GEORGE JORDEN was an ardent lover of nature, and with the very least external advantages gradually acquired such a thorough acquaintance with the natural history of the neighbourhood that his opinion was asked for and respected by some of the most learned men in England. He was born on the Clee Hills in the parish of Farlow, where his father was a labourer, and his mother a herb-doctress. He came to Bewdley as an errand boy, taught himself to read and write, and soon afterwards went to live with Mr. Fryer (abovementioned), with whom he remained for 50 years. Being favoured with a sympathetic master he was able to follow his natural bent with unwearied assiduity. Rising before daylight he spent some hours among his flowers in the Forest, of which he is said to have known "every inch," and came back loaded with specimens for his herbarium, in time to begin his day's work at home. A monument of his diligence is left in his "Flora Bellus Locus," now in the Worcester Museum, and in his herbarium of beautifully mounted specimens now in the possession of Mr. Gabb. He collected, mounted, and named probably every plant which grows wild within ten miles of Bewdley; and he is specially mentioned by Mr. W. A. Leighton in his *Flora of Shropshire* and by Mr. Edwin Lees, F.L.S., in his *Botany of Worcestershire* as having rendered them most effectual aid. He also accumulated a mass of local antiquarian lore, including old ballads and electioneering songs, which he bequeathed to the Worcester Museum. He died in 1871, aged 88.

EDWARD BAUGH, son of the Rev. E. Baugh, minister of St. Anne's, was also a zealous Bewdley naturalist. He made a large collection of specimens illustrating the geology of the neighbourhood, and many of these are now in the British

Museum. The remainder, with cases, have been presented to the Bewdley Institute by Mrs. T. Baugh, and when arranged they will form the nucleus of a good local museum.

JOHN TIBBITTS published a volume of *Poems* in 1811. The greater part of the book is taken up with descriptions of Bewdley and Spring Grove. The metre is somewhat peculiar, but the sentiments are good and the narrative is interesting.

SAMUEL SKEY was a native of Upton-on-Severn, and was apprenticed to a grocer in Bewdley named Church. When he had finished his apprenticeship £1000 was left to him by a relation, and with this he began business as a grocer and drysalter in Bewdley.* He afterwards erected large chemical works in Dowles, chiefly for the manufacture of sulphuric and nitric acids. His enterprises succeeded, and he became a very wealthy man. He then determined to build himself a house on a spot called Jacky-stone hill in Wribbenhall. When he sought to purchase the land he found it was entailed; but nothing daunted, he obtained a special Act of Parliament "for vesting part of the devised estates of Thomas Lord Foley in Samuel Skey in fee simple in exchange for another estate of equal value." The pools called the "Slashes" on Kidderminster Common, and Warren Heath, were made over to Skey in exchange for farms in Bromsgrove and Upton Warren (1775). The rough estate thus acquired was tastefully laid out and planted; and now forms the beautiful grounds of Spring Grove. The house was commenced in 1787, and first inhabited in 1790. Mr. Skey was buried at Dowles, July 29, 1812. About 1850 the Spring Grove estate was purchased by Mr. Walter C. Hemming.

GEORGE GRIFFITH served his first clerkship in a corn-merchant's office in Bewdley. He devoted his leisure to self-culture; and quite early in life became possessed with two ruling passions—verse making, and the reformation of grammar schools. His writings were very voluminous, chiefly in "history, history-romance, drama, satire, and a miscellaneous worship of the Muse." His chief publications were *The Free Schools of Worcestershire*, *Life of George Wilson*, *Going to Markets and Grammar Schools*, and *Records in the Midland Counties*. He died in 1883, and was buried at Ribbesford.

* Nicholls' *Lecture on Bewdley*.

Ribbesford.

THE oldest relic of human habitation in this parish is a celt of greenish stone found in the bed of the river while digging for gravel. It is of the Neolithic period; and one end has a maul, the other an axe. It is delineated in Evans's *Flint Implements* and in Allies' *Antiquities of Worcestershire.*

The earliest written record of Ribbesford is contained in an Anglo-Saxon charter belonging to Lord Somers, and printed at the end of Heming's *Chartal. Eccles. Wigorn.* (page 598). It is entitled "Contract of *Wulfstan* Archbishop of York & also Bishop of Worcester to give *Ribbedforde* [&c.] to his Sister for her life—then to be married to *Wulfric.*"

"Here is set forth in this writing, concerning those Agreements which *Wulfric* & the Archbishop made when he obtained the Archbishop's sister [to] him to wife. That is, that he promised her that land at *Ealretune* and at *Ribbedforda* [for] her day. And he promised her that land at *Cnihte-wican* [Knightwick]; that he would have her hold it three men's day at [of] that family [Convent] in *Wincelcumbe* [Winchcombe]: & gave her that land of *Eanulfintune* to give & to grant to whom she chose in [her] day, and after [her] day, there [where] her best liking was: & promised her 50 mancs* of gold & 30 men & 30 horses.

"Now was to these a witness *Wulfstan* Archbishop, & *Leofwine* Alderman, & *Athelstan* Bishop, & *Alfword* Abbot, and *Brihtch* Monk, and many a good man to increase them, both consecrated & lay, that these agreements were thus made. Now are to these agreements two Writings, the one with the Archbishop in *Wigerceastre* & the other with *Aethelstane* Bishop in *Hereford.*"

---

* A manc was worth about 7*s.* 6*d.*

The holy man, who thus portioned his sister with the goods of the Church, held the sees of York and Worcester from 1002 to 1023. Wulfstan's nephew Brithlege was his next successor but one in the see of Worcester; and if he was *this* sister's son, the transaction above-mentioned must have occurred soon after his promotion, for Brithlege succeeded in 1033. Wulfstan was surnamed "Reprobate." *Nam nimis erravit, dum rebus nos spoliavit*—"For he erred too much when he spoiled us of our possessions," said the Monks. He was also surnamed Lupus or "The Wolf," and a spirited address of his to the English, when they were hard pressed by the Danes, is still extant.* Wulfric's enjoyment of Ribbesford would hardly have ceased before the Danes came over. In 1002, Sept. 13, the Danes throughout England were murdered by order of King Ethelred. Sweyn, King of Denmark, came to exact vengeance, and within a few years his son Canute gained the sovereignty of the land. Earl Hacun, a Dane, took Clifton, Eastham, and Tenbury from Worcester Monastery; and other Danes seized Ribbesford. With more settled times the Monks recovered Ribbesford; and the villagers were bound to provide them with fishing nets and hunting tackle whenever required to do so. Again, however, misfortune befel the monks, and after the Norman Conquest Turstin, a Fleming, deprived them of their rights here.† Though Turstin appears here as guilty of sacrilege, yet, as we have already seen, he gave Wrubenhale (Bewdley) to the Priory of Worcester. Turstin married Agnes daughter of Alured, a great landowner in Herefordshire and Wiltshire. Agnes held Cuure (Cowarne Magna) and a large manor unnamed at time of Domesday.‡ William FitzOsborn, Earl of Hereford, gave the manors of Duntune (Downton Castle) in Herefordshire, and Mawley and Cleobury in Shropshire, to Turstinus Flandrensis.

* It is printed in Sweet's *Anglo-Saxon Reader*, pp. 102-111.

† *De Ribetforde.*—Simili modo villam quæ Ribbetford dicitur, cujus villani captatorias sepes piscium et alias venatorias instaurare debita lege debebant, operaque nostra, ubicunque eis precipiebatur, exercebant, prius Dani, post Turstanus Flandrensis monasterio vi abstulit, sicque ejus nunc dominatum perdidimus, ipseque non multo post et ipsam et omnem terram suam perdidit, exilioque multatus est. Sic qui parum Deo injustè abstulit, omnia sua justè perdidit."—Heming's *Chart*, fol. 120, Hearne's Ed. Oxford, 1723, vol. 1, p. 256; and *Monasticon* i., 594.

‡ Eyton's *Shropshire*, v., 74.

In 1074 Roger Earl of Hereford (son of Earl William) rebelled against the Conqueror, but was defeated, and condemned to perpetual imprisonment and to forfeiture of all his property. Turstin was probably concerned in this outbreak, and when it failed he lost not only Ribbesford but all his other estates, and was banished from the country. "And so," says the monkish chronicler, "he who unjustly took away a little from God, justly lost all his own property."

Agnes the widow of Turstin Flandrensis, and his son Eustace a knight, lord of Witteney, gave land to the church of St. Peter at Gloucester.

After the forfeiture of Roger Earl of Hereford his lands of Wigmore, Cleobury, &c. were given to Ralph de Mortimer. Ribbesford also came into the possession of the Mortimers, and was held under them by a knightly family who resided there, and who from it took their name of "de Ribbesford."

Walter de Ribesford was present at the inquisition taken about Oswaldslow Hundred in the time of John de Pageham, Bishop of Worcester (1151—1158).* Mr. Hayley thinks that he was the same person mentioned by Camden *(Brit.,* 733) under the name of Gualterus de Ridensford who went with Richard Strongbow, Earl of Pembroke, to assist Dermot Mac Morrough in Ireland. Lord Lyttelton in his *Life of Henry II.* (vol. iii., p. 73) says, "John the furious after making a very brave defence was honorably slain upon the field of battle by Walter de Riddelsford, an English knight, & the horsemen of his troop." It appears, however, very doubtful whether Ribbesford can claim the honour of this exploit.

Maud, daughter of Sir John Ribbesford, Kt., was wife of Henry de Temple, of Temple, Leicestershire, *temp.* Henry II.†

In 4th John (1203) "Simon de Ribbeford r. c. (fined) de x marcis ne transfretet at Rogerum de Toni ad reddendum compotum quem ab eo exegit."‡

* Heming's *Cart.*, 291.

† Collins' *Peerage*, 4th Edw., v. 6, p. 45.

‡ Madox's *Hist. of the Exchq.*, i., 505.

Ribbesford House

From an old Oil Painting.

Whiteman & Bass Photo Litho London

In 1236 Henry de Ripeford, in the county of Worcester, paid xxs. for three parts of a fief, held of Ralph de Mortimer, as an aid at the marriage of Isabella, sister of Henry III., to the Emperor of Germany.*

Simon de Ribefort was one of four knights appointed in 42 Henry III. to inquire into grievances, &c., in the county of Worcester.† This was done in conformity with the "Provisions of Oxford" enacted under the influence of the famous Simon de Montfort, and was the commencement of County Members. From the Blakeway MS. we learn that this "Simon de Rybbeford by deed conceded to his Lord Roger de Mortimer all the right which he had to hunt in his wood of Rybbeford which is called *La Hoke;* nor would he pursue any sort of wild beasts in the forest of Wyre without special leave from the aforesaid Lord Roger or his heirs, under forfeiture of all he held under the same Lord Roger, or that his heirs should hold, for ever. Saving to himself during his life, that if he should be hunting in any of his parks and woods besides *La Hoke*, and his dogs should run any beast from his parks or woods into the forest of Wyre, and follow it, contrary to his wishes—the transgression, if it can be so called, should be settled by the arbitration of friends.

"Witnesses. "William de Beauchamp
"Thomas, Rector of the Church of Rybbeford
"Nicholas, Rector (? ranger) of the forest
"Jacob his brother
"William son of Guarini
"William Corbett
"William Le Poer."

This transaction took place sometime between 1247 and 1269; and the desire to secure additional hunting-grounds in the neighbourhood confirms the opinion that about this time the Mortimers built an occasional residence for the family at Ticknell.

King Edward I. in 1306, for augmenting the glory of his intended expedition into Scotland, did at Whitsuntide begirt Edward Earl of Carnarvon his eldest son, with the military belt; and thereupon the young prince immediately at the high

* *Testa de Nevill*, p. 40.

† App. to Bindy's *Hist. Eng.* 224 Pat., 42 Hen. III.

altar in Westminster Abbey conferred the honour of knighthood on 300 more, sons of Earls, Barons, and Knights, who attended the King to Scotland. Amongst those so distinguished was Henry de Rypsford. His arms were *ermine, a chief gules fretty or.* In 1310, 1318, and 1328 Sir Henry presented to the Rectory of Ribbesford. In the *Calendarium Rotulorum Chartarum*, 2 Edw. III. (1329), page 160, his possessions are enumerated as follows:—"Rookes (Rock) maner' mercat' feria; Snede; La Clouse; Ribbeford; Houke; Waskerige; Linden Coudray; all having free warren." A deed in the possession of S. Z. Lloyd, Esq., of Areley Hall—undated, but probably about the time of Edward II.—sets forth that Godith, widow of Osbert de Wetacre, had conveyed to Simon de Ribbesford certain land, with the precincts thereof, situated in *Hultonestrete* (Hylton Street), in Worcester. In 1349 Robert de Ribbesford presented to the rectory of the church.

In 1364 Constance, wife of Walter de Ribbesford, had the manor of Ribbesford assigned for her dower.* The possessions of Walter in 1371 are set down as Ribbesford manor; La Rooks—two small pieces of land *(due pecie terr')*; and Wigemore *(sect' cur')*.†

The Ribbesfords remained here certainly till 2 Henry VI.; but the presentation to the living, and probably the ownership of the manor, had before that time passed into the hands of the Beauchamps. In 1387 Thomas de Beauchamp, Earl of Warwick, appears as patron of the church.

In 21 Rd. II (1398), Sir John de Montacute, Earl of Salisbury, obtained from the King a grant to himself of the manors of Shrawley Roke and Ribbesford *in Com. Wig.*, with the advowsons of the churches of the said manors, then seized into the King's hands by the attainder of Thos. Beauchamp, Earl of Warwick.‡ On the deposition of Richard II. these lands were probably restored to the Beauchamps, for Margaret, widow of Earl Thomas, held it at her death in 1407.§ In 1446 Henry Beauchamp, Earl of Warwick, owned both manor

* *Inquis. post Mortem*, vol. iv., p. 271.

† *Inquis. post Mortem*, vol. iv., p. 305.

‡ Collins' *Peerage*, vol. ii., p. 68.

§ *Inquis. post Mortem*, vol. iii., p. 312.

and advowson.* His only child Anne died three years after her father, and the ownership then went to Anne Countess of Warwick, wife of Richard Nevil, the famous Kingmaker. The next heir was Margaret, wife of John Talbot, Earl of Shrewsbury, the "Terror of France." From her it descended to the Viscounts Lisle. In the time of Henry VII. it came to Elizabeth, wife of Edmund Dudley, memorable in history as a partner in the firm of "Empson and Dudley." Her son, the last owner of Ribbesford by descent from the Beauchamps, was the famous John Dudley, father-in-law of the Lady Jane Grey, created Duke of Northumberland by Edward VI. After the execution of Northumberland his estates were forfeited, and Ribbesford was granted to Sir Robert Acton, Kt., whose son sold it to the Churchills. It soon passed by purchase to Sir Robert Cooke, then to Sir Henry Mildmay, and afterwards to Sir Henry Herbert, in whose family it remained for exactly 160 years. Sir Henry Herbert, Kt., Master of the Revels, made the purchase in 1627; and among the persons named in the deed of conveyance was his brother George Herbert, the saintly poet of the English Church. Sir Henry Herbert's name appears often in the Appendix, and he was a generous benefactor to Ribbesford. In 1640 he was elected to the "Long Parliament" as Member for Bewdley; but on Aug. 20, 1642, the House of Commons resolved that he should be disabled from sitting on account of his having put into execution the King's Commission of Array. At the Restoration he was again returned for Bewdley, and held the seat until his death in 1673. His son Henry was returned for Bewdley in 1676; and in 1694 he was created Baron Herbert of Cherbury, in consequence of the failure of male issue in the elder branch of the family. His son Henry succeeded as Lord Herbert of Cherbury in 1708, and was Recorder of Bewdley. In 1738, however, he committed suicide by hanging in one of the turrets of Ribbesford House.† Having no issue, the title became extinct, and the manor passed to his cousin, Henry Morley, a descendant of Sir Henry Herbert. In 1782 the estate was inherited by George

* *Inquis. post Mortem*, vol. iv., p. 230.

† It is said that his valet came into the room while Lord Herbert was still living, but not daring to thwart so great a man, he ran off to Bewdley to ask the Bailiff what was to be done!

Paulet, afterwards Marquis of Winchester, who in 1787 sold the same to Francis Ingram, of Ticknell. Mr. Ingram died Oct. 21, 1797, and by will gave the estate to Sir E. Winnington, Bart., of Stanford Court, for his life; and after his decease to Edward Winnington, the second son of the said Sir E. Winnington, and his first and other sons in succession, he and they taking and using the name and arms of Ingram. The present owner is the Rev. E. Winnington Ingram, Rector of Stanford-on-Teme.

The house is of great antiquity, and doubtless stands on the spot occupied by the de Ribbesfords in the time of Henry II. It was formerly turreted, with a moat round it, over which by a drawbridge a spacious court-yard was entered. The arms of Herbert with motto "Pawb yn y arver" are over a doorway. About 1790 two sides of the quadrangle were pulled down, and the moat filled up. In 1830 several thousand pounds were spent in repairing and improving the house.

The church, dedicated to St. Leonard, is in parts very old, and is especially remarkable for its wooden arcade separating the nave from the south aisle.* The original church here was of the Norman period, and was only a small chapel occupying about two-thirds of the north aisle. Mr. Loftus Brock has traced out the growth of the church. He says, "Probably the first enlargement took place eastward, the north wall of the nave being carried on in a straight line, and so assuming its present length and position. The next enlargement was probably the present nave of the church, the south aisle being evidently a still later addition. The extension of the church to include the present nave was doubtless made sometime in the first half of the 15th century, and might very possibly coincide with the time when Henry VI. put the town of Bewdley into the parish of Ribbesford."

In the south aisle is a little door which leads by a winding staircase to the entrance of what was formerly the roodloft. Under the roodloft was the carved oak rood screen, of which some interesting pieces are now preserved in the pulpit. In one compartment is a fox, dressed like a monk, preaching to a

* There were formerly two wooden arcades, and the church would then resemble the very interesting one at Lower Peover, near Northwich, Cheshire, which has not undergone much change since the time of Henry VI.

congregation of geese. Another represents a pig playing the bagpipes, while the little pigs dance to the music. These are probably caricatures of the begging friars, between whom and the parish priests there was often much bitterness.

Here the greatest puzzle to antiquaries is a rude shallow carving on the tympanum over the north door. It belongs to the earliest part of the Norman period, and is in a good state of preservation. The illustration of it is from a sketch by "Cuthbert Bede," who was the first to clear away the thick coats of

whitewash from some of the smaller carvings on this doorway. The question is, What was in the mind of the sculptor when he made it? Was it to commemorate an event in local history, or was it an emblem of the Christian faith? There are some curious local legends connected with the figure of the Archer Knight; but the latter is the more probable view, especially as so many unmistakably ecclesiastical carvings were made about the same time in other churches.* The Gospel was to be preached to an uneducated people "*in* churches indeed pre-eminently, but also *by* churches subordinately," and purely *secular* subjects are rarely if ever seen on sacred buildings of this date. On Ribbesford porch we have a rude but clear emblem of our Redemption. The human soul, personified by the deer or other animal, is fleeing from the pursuit of a huge monster—typical of the evil one—when the Saviour intervenes, and slays the enemy. In Norman times the Archer would be the most real symbol of strength. This, too, seems to be the teaching of the carving on one of the capitals. A bird is swooping down on a fish. Coming to the rescue, however, is a larger bird, which in turn swoops down upon the robber and delivers the fish. The fact of the final safety of the fish is shown by its re-appearing above. Now the fish is the well-known emblem of the Christian. Tertullian says: "For we after our Lord and Saviour Jesus Christ, our Ιχθυς, are also fishes, and born in the water, nor are we otherwise saved but by remaining in the water." On the font in Castle Frome church, Herefordshire, is the ecclesiastical representation of Christians under the form of little fishes, surrounding the figure of Christ in the waters of Baptism.

The church was thoroughly restored in 1878 at a cost of nearly £4000, and on removing the coats of plaster it was found that about 400 years ago the walls had been decorated with fresco-painting. In the time of Edward VI. this was whitewashed over, and texts of Scripture were painted on the walls. These texts in their turn were whitewashed; and then again came texts of the time of Elizabeth and James I.

During the restoration two monumental stones were also brought to light which had covered the remains of those who occupied a high position in the society of former days. The Rev. Prebendary F. T. Havergal describes them thus:—"No. 1 is a fine coped grey sandstone, nearly perfect, about

* On the Norman tympanum of Aston church, Herefordshire (see frontispiece *Diocesan Calendar*, 1883), is a representation of the Lamb with a cross, the Ox and the Eagle—all well-known Christian emblems. "At Luton, Beds, on the font is a lamb guarding a vine from the attacks of a dragon. At Thorpe Arnold, Leicestershire, appears a Christian soldier, opposing a shield bearing a cross to the attacks of fiery serpents who assault him in vain, thus guarded." *(Ayliffe Poole: Churches*, p. 45.) Instances of this kind might be rapidly multiplied.

six feet six inches long. The foliated cross is of the kind commonly adopted at the period. The date may safely be assigned to the latter part of century XIII., probably placed over the body of an incumbent of this church. The hollow chamfer down each side is an unusual feature, and the staff on the top of the stone, being grasped by two hands, is a mode of treatment I have never seen before. No. II is part of an incised stone coffin lid of a layman in two pieces. [It had been built into the east wall of the S. aisle.] In all respects this is a most interesting fragment: all its details plainly indicate that it is the work of the former part of century XIV.—*circa* 1310 to 1320. The inscriptions were usually in rhyme. The use of three circular stops between each word is a distinct characteristic of this period." [The inscription has been mentioned on page 4.] Habingdon gives a description of monuments, &c., in this church about 1630. The Mortimer and Beauchamp arms are broken. In the N. window of the church the arms of *Ribbesford:* Ermine a chief gu. fretted or. In the E. window of the chancel and highest pane, Gules seven mascles or. Quincy, *Earl of Winchester;* quartering Azure, a mullet argent pierced of the field. The second and third quarters of the escutcheon defaced. The fourth as the first. In the dexter pane below, *Mortimer* with an escutcheon arg. quartering or, a cross gu. *Ulster.* In the sinister, Gu. a fesse between six cross crosslets or. *Beauchamp, Earl of Warwick.* In the N. window of the chancel the keeper of a forest praying: FILI DEI, MISERERE MEI. Behind him his son; next his wife praying, O MATER DEI MEMENTO MEI; after her four daughters: the subscription, ORATE PRO ANIMABUS ROBERTI BORSELEPOLE ET MARGARETÆ UXORIS EJUS. Over them a man praying, FILI DEI, MISERERE MEI; and his wife in like sort praying, MATER DEI MEMENTO MEI: the subscription, ORATE PRO ANIMABUS PETRI GANSOR ET MARGARETÆ UXORIS EJUS. In the sinister pane of the south window of the chancel, Gu. in chief or, a lion passant sable; Sir David Veryett or Howell or Dymotte (for these three carried this coat) quartering Arg. three eaglets displayed sable: the subscription, ORATE PRO ANIMAB[s], the rest broken out. In the E. window of N. aisle, France and England quarterly with a file of three labels arg.; in the second pane, *Beauchamp* quartering *Warwick;* under the first, Or a chevron gules and quarter ermine; under the second, Arg. on a bend azure three cinque foils or. In the second N. window a gentleman armed and praying: on his coat armour, Gironné of twelve arg. and gules (Peverell).* In the second pane a man with his wife and daughter, all praying; his name *Hayles*, his wife's *Margeria*. In the highest S. window the grocers' arms; under them the benefactors', of whom only *Roger Wear* and *Ann*, his wife, remain. In the second S. window, France and England quarterly,* with the names of the following benefactors:—*Woddall*, *Southall*, *Thomas Haylls*, and *Alice*, his wife; the rest broken. In the W. window, *Waldecote*, a benefactor. In the chancel is a table of the arms of Russel of Strensham. The crest, on a wreath argent and sable, a demi lion argent, coloured sable, studded or, holding a cross cruselée botonné fitchée sable. Another crest argent a plume of feathers or and azure. On a wall in the S. aisle the arms of Herbert quartering (1) Earl of Hereford, (2) Newmarch, (3) Semarche, (4) Newton), (5) Hylton, (6) Morgan. In the N. aisle an ancient monument of a man and his wife quite worn out. Some monuments in the S. aisle with crosses. On one of them—"Charles Acton, son of Henry Acton."

On the E. wall of chancel (now on wall of S. aisle):—John Tiler late Bailiffe of Bewdley 28 Jan. 1626; Joan his wife died 1628.

Elizabeth wife of John Boraston died 13 Dec. 1662.

On an alabaster monument are the names of the following persons (among others) whose bodies were interred near the middle of the chancel:—John Soley gent. 4 June 1604. Margaret his wife 5 Jan. 1639. John Soley gent. their son 17 Feb. 1652 aged 60. John Soley his son 20 April 1665 aged 63. John Soley of Samborn in this county Esq. 17 Oct. 1730 aged 54.

On other stones are memorials of the following persons:—

John Boraston sometime prebendary of Hereford & Rector of this church fifty-eight years with the chapel of Bewdley annexed 29 Dec. 1688 aged 85.

John Addenbroke gent. 3 Feb. 1663. Mrs Margaret Addenbroke, dr of Mr Edward Addenbroke, late Rector of Lower Sapey, and brother to John Addenbroke above-mentioned 4 April 1712 aged 29.

William Price, Rector of Ribbesford, 26 Sept. 1724 aged 60.

James Perkes senior freeman of Bewdley 23 April 1710.

Richard Clare 11 Jan. 1708 aged 53.

John Pooler rector of Ribbesford 11 Aug. 1706 aged 39.

* These arms are now in the south window of the west end.

Ribbesford.

Ribbesford.

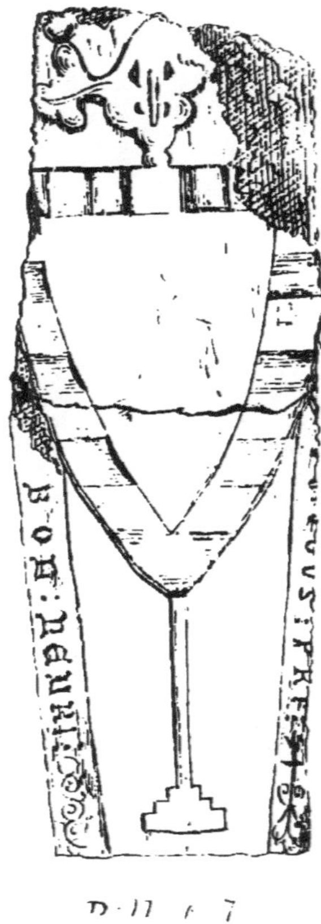

Walter de Balun, Upper Arley.

Richard Cheeke gent. & Mary his wife (only dr of Sam. Jones gent.) he died 27 May, 1754 aged 39.

"Here lie interred the bodies of William Hopkins late of Bewdley gent. who deceased July 19, 1647 And Helena his wife who deceased Nov. 16, 1656 both in a good old age.

Ask you in these what vertues were
Needlesse it is to write them here
Go ask the rich they know full well
Or ask the poor for they can tell.
G. H. posuit.

"Joh. Cupper Cler. Gram. Scholæ Liberæ de Bewdley Proto Magister in expectatione diei supremi qualis erat dies iste indicabit Ob 27 Jan. A.D. 1720 Aetat. Suæ 57."

Mr Burnd Westlake d. 24 Jan. 1742 aged 42.

Benj. Beale merchant 29 May 1745.

Benj. Beale, merchant 20 Feb. 1786.

Susanna Beale married Paul Hughes of Kidderminster Esq. d. 14 Jan. 1868 aged 95.

Bonham Caldwell d. 13 Feb. 1797.

On the wall of S. aisle is a handsome brass, which was erected by the officers of the Inniskillen Dragoons to the memory of Captain F. W. Ingram, son of the Rev. E. W. Ingram, Rector of Ribbesford.

"Lt. Col. Thomas Onslow Winnington Ingram third son of Rev. E. W. Ingram of Ribbesford House. He was killed at Lucknow in the East Indies March 14th 1858 when in command of his regiment at the capture of the Kaiserbagh in the 42nd year of his age."

Marianne Elizabeth wife of Rev. John Ryle Wood Canon of Worcester & youngest daughter of Rev. E. W. Ingram. Born at Ribbesford June 8, 1824, d. at Worcester Aug. 10, 1844.

Rev. E. W. Ingram Canon of Worcester Cathedral and for 32 years Rector of this parish d. May 7 1851 aged 65. Jane his wife dr. of the Very Rev. Arthur Onslow D.D. Dean of Worcester d. Dec. 10 1850 aged 66.

Mr John Hayley Alderman of Bewdley Oct. 1 1779 ætat 57.

Rev. John Hayley Jan. 16 1795 ætat 36.

Margaret wife of Thomas Hayley 19th Sept. 1812 aged 41.

Thomas Hayley 28 March 1821 aged 61.

Frances his second wife 19 June 1832 aged 54.

James Fryer, Esq., of Bewdley, who died 27 Feb., 1856, aged 87 years. He followed the medical profession with honor to himself and benefit to others, and by his will bequeathed, amongst other charitable legacies, £2000 to the Bewdley National School, £4000 to the Worcester Infirmary, and £900 for the benefit of Bewdley Forest Church.

Christopher Bancks 30 March 1788 aged 67.

Reader.

Let not the allurements of a corrupted world seduce thee from the path that leads to Glory and immortality. The bed of death will not then be a scene of Terror nor thy last Hour an Hour of Despair.

James Bancks son of the above 13 June 1810.

Christopher son of William Bancks Feb. 10 1834 aged 79.

William son of Robert Bancks of Wigan June 7 1793 aged 70.

Margaret Bancks July 2, 1858 aged 86.

Peggy wife of the late William Bancks of Corbyns Hall Staffs. Aug. 14, 1810 aged 54.

There is still left a fine representation in old stained glass of St. George and the dragon. The arms of France and England quarterly with two falcons as supporters are also entire. [Richard Duke of York or Edward IV.] A window representing the Ascension was erected in 1870 in memory of Adam Prattinton and Ellen Brook his wife. There is also a beautiful memorial window designed by Burne Jones "To the Glory of God and in memory of Hannah Macdonald, Bewdley, widow, who died March 7, 1875, aged 66." This window was erected by Alfred Baldwin, Esq., of Wilden House.

There are some curious specimens of churchyard poetry, among which are the following relating to the Severn bargemen:—

"My anchor's cast—
My rope's on shore—
And here I lie
Till time's no more."

John Oakes, Dec. 23, 1821, aged 27.
"Boreas' blast and Neptune's waves
Have tossed me to and fro;
I strove all I could my life to save;
At last obliged to go.
Now at an anchor here I lay,
Wher's many of the fleet;
But now once more must I set sail
My Saviour Christ to meet."

"Mary, I could wait the wind night and day:
Through Severn's dangerous course I've made my way
Full forty years, in friendship's trusty bark,
Guided by Providence in light and dark,
With future hopes of being for ever blest:
So my friends adieu:
Here I lie at rest."

List of Rectors and Patrons of Ribbesford.

Patrons.	Incumbents. (With Date of Institution).
Sir Henry de Ribbesford	Simon de Ribbesford, 1 Dec., 1310 William de Piryton, 15 Nov., 1318 Gilbert the Granger of Northlech, 12 April, 1328
Robert de Ribbesford	John Bray, 5 May, 1349
Thos. Beauchamp, Earl of Warwick.	Walter Elyot, 1 April, 1387
Henry Beauchamp, Earl of Warwick	Richard Hyde, 31 July, 1444
William Herbert, of Herbert and of Pembroke, by grant of the King	David Gibbes, 28 Oct., 1467
Thomas Blount, by grant of John Viscount Lisle	Walter Blount, LL.B., 7 March, 1507
Robert Acton, Esq.	David Couper, M.A., 24 May, 1531 Richard Shute, 25 Oct., 1538
Sir Robert Acton, Kt.	Thomas Hopkins, 26 June, 1544
Robert Acton, Esq.	John Lewis, *alias* Duke, 18 Nov., 1556
?	George Sowthall, B.A., 17 Jan., 1600*
William Cooke, Esq.	John Hamond, B.A., 2 March, 1614
King Charles I. (by lapse)	John Boraston, M.A., 4 March, 1630
Henry Herbert, Esq.	Anthony Lucas, 7 March, 1688
Henry, Lord Herbert of Cherbury	John Pooler, M.A., 10 July, 1695 William Price, 18 Feb., 1706 John Bradley, B.A., 20 April, 1725 Thomas Knight, M.A., 10 March, 1730
Henry Arthur, Earl of Powis	Edward Baugh, M.A., 19 April, 1765
George Paulet, Esq.	William Jesse, M.A., 27 Aug., 1795
Thomas Ingram, Esq.	Edward Winnington Ingram, M.A., 31 Jan., 1815
Rev. Edward Winnington Ingram	E. W. Ingram, M.A., 4 Dec., 1847
Rev. E. W. Ingram	John Walcot, M.A., 14 July, 1854 E. H. W. Ingram, M.A., 13 March, 1876

---

* Date of induction; date of institution not known.

Dowles.

OWLES takes its name from the brook which here enters the Severn: it is derived from the Celtic *dhu*, black, which still appears in five rivers in Wales called Dulas.* For the early history of Dowles we are indebted to the laborious investigations made by the late Rev. R. W. Eyton, the historian of Shropshire. "Dowles," he says,† "is cut off from Stottesden by eight miles of intervening territory, and by the Forest of Wyre, a not insignificant barrier. But Dowles, isolated and distant, was yet under another name a member of the *Domesday* manor of Stottesden. Its ancient name was Achisey or Hakieshey. Either one of the Palatine Earls or else Henry I. granted it to Wydo son of Helgot at a *ferm* or rent of 2*s.* per annum. Helgot was Domesday Lord of Stanton and the Founder of Castle Holgate. Wydo, the second of three sons, had three estates, at Quat, Achiseia, and in Worcestershire. Previous to 1127 he granted them all to Great Malvern Priory. Henry I. being at Hereford in 1126 or 1127 confirmed to Malvern *inter alia* those two *solidates* of land, 'that is Achescia, which pertains to Stottesdun, for which Wido Fitz Helgot used to render 2*s.* per annum of *ferm*.' He also concedes it to them 'quit of those 2*s.* and of all other services, for the health of his soul.' In consequence of the King's quittance of his rent, the Sheriffs of Shropshire for ages deducted from their annual *ferms* a sum of 2*s.* in alms to the Monks of Malvern: thus, 'In elemosynis constitutis Monachis de Malvern 2*s.*'"

---

* Isaac Taylor's *Words and Places*, p. 143.

† Eyton's *Shropshire*, vol. iv., p. 160.

Henry's Winchester Charter of 1127 shows that Achisey was the present Dowles. The King is reciting a grant he had made of land on the east of Severn, and perhaps a part of the royal manor of Kidderminster. He uses these words: "I give them also the land of Northw'* to assart between Hauckesbroc and Lindrugesithe from Heneduneia to the Severn, to hold quietly and freely for ever." He then adds, "And on the other side of the Severn I give them 2 *solidates* of land, that is Hakiesheia, together with a certain part of the wood which pertained unto Stottesd', according to those bounds whereof Fulco, the Sheriff, has caused perambulation to be made, which Fulco hath seized them (the Monks) thereof by my command; & this land I allow to be free of the said 2*s.* & of all other services."

"Of Dowles under its new name, and as a possession of Malvern Priory," continues Eyton, "we hear nothing for 2 centuries. In Oct., 1292, the Prior of Great Malvern was sued under *quo warranto* for his right of holding *pleas of the Crown*, of seizing the chattels of his men when *fugitive* or convicted (of felony), and of having *wayf* in his manor of Doules. The Prior appeared and cited Henry III.'s Charter to Westminster Abbey and its Cells (of which Malvern was one). He said he held two great Courts yearly. The matter went to a jury, which found that the Prior had never held the said two Courts, nor tried any pleas of the Crown till 3 years back, when he obliged his men of Doules to cross the Severn and attend his Court of Nortwode in Wors^e^. The suit of Court thus lost to the Crown they valued at 2*s.* per annum. So on this point the Prior was *in misericordia*: he forfeited the said suits and their appurtenant franchises, which remained to the King, and had to pay 6*s.* damages for the 3 years above-mentioned. Afterwards the Judges conceded the disputed Courts to the Prior for an annual rent of 6*s.* 8*d.* if the King would accept it. As to chattels and wayf, two clauses of the Charter warranted the Prior's claim."

The taxation of 1291 omits Malvern's interest in Dowles, unless a *carucate* of land at Northwood and 20*s.* of *assized rent* there can include both estates.

---

* Northwood east of Severn exactly opposite Dowles Wood on the west bank. Hawkeshay and Hawkesbrook are perhaps connected in nomenclature with Hawkbatch.

Richard le Wireman granted and confirmed to Edmund de Mortimer a weir at Dowles with a fishery, which had been held by him of the Prior and Convent of Great Malvern, he paying to the Convent 10*s.* in silver and to the chief lord of Kidderminster 2*s.* Witnesses—Henry de Rybbeford, Ralph de Arrag., Hugo de ffrene, William de Foxcote.

In 1534 Dowles and Northwood are collectively valued as a Shropshire estate of Malvern Priory. The *assized* rents and rents of tenants-at-will were £9 18*s.* 9*d.*; the fines, heriots, and amercements of Court were 10*s.*; the average profits from the Wood, £1; the total of £11 8*s.* 9*d.* was lessened by 10*s.*, the annual value of some structure (*Kidellus*, a kiddle or kettle, a contrivance for catching fish set in a weir) in the Severn which had been destroyed by the King's order. The *Ministers' Accounts* of 1542-3 give a total of £12 15*s.* 6½*d.* as arising from similar sources, but mention Dowles only as the estate thus valued. (*Monasticon* III., p. 453.)

Eyton says it is difficult to conjecture how Dowles church came to exist. If it had been built *before* the manor passed to Malvern it would have been affiliated to Stottesden. The monks did not willingly found churches, though they readily appropriated them. This may be an exception. More singularly, it was never appropriated by the monks, but remained a Rectory! It was formerly dedicated to St. Lawrence.* After the Reformation it appears as St. Andrew's.† The *Valor* of 1534 gives Rectory of Dowlyz as in Deanery of Burford—£4 per annum in glebe and tithes; Thomas Blakwey, Incumbent. The Priory of Great Malvern had a pension of 13*s.* 4*d.* therefrom. (*Val. Eccl.* III., 214, 240.)

At the suppression of the monasteries Dowles and Lilleshall Abbey were given to James Leveson, "marchant of the Staple of Caleys."‡ "By indenture 17 Aug. 35 Henry VIII. (1543) James Leveson conveys to Thomas Grey of Whyttington Staffs. the Manor & Lordship of Dowles with all the rights &c. to the late Priorie of *Moche Malverne* late belonging and appertaining,

* 1514. A brief for St. Lawrence of Dowles.

† Ecton's *Thesaurus*, 1742. Bacon's *Liber Regis*, 1786.

‡ An ancestor of the Duke of Sutherland and Earl Granville.

y[t] is to whytt :—Hollowfeld. The Were, Holly days. Drayford. The Holleyn. Cotes. The Grove lode. Milwardes. Crabbes. Botts. Trynyte Ground. Corkerells. With the Advowson of the Church—all which were given by letters patent to James Levison dated 14 July 35 Henry VIII." Consideration £320. An annuity of 26*s*. 8*d*. was to be given to John and Thomas Greene, Bailiffs of the Manor of Dowles. The seal is of red wax. Crest, a goat's head.

About 1570 Francis Newport, Esq., appears to have been the owner, and the manor remained in his family more than 100 years, for in 1661 and 1669 Francis Lord Newport presented to the Rectory. In 1677 Henry Herbert, Esq., of Ribbesford House (afterwards Lord Herbert of Cherbury), married Anne Ramsay and £5000 of her dowry was settled upon her, and Dowles was bought with the money. This explains why Lord Herbert of Cherbury was called upon in 1695 to arbitrate about the right to certain "kneelings" in Dowles church.* About 1790 the manor was purchased by Samuel Skey, Esq., the builder of Spring Grove, who set up extensive chemical works in the parish. A tramway and canal that he constructed are still to be traced, leading to the spot where the present Gasworks stand. There were also extensive brass and pewter works, and gold refining was carried on. Dowles continued in the hands of the Skey family till 1871, when it was purchased by the late Edward Pease, Esq., of Darlington.

The old stone church, built soon after the time of Henry II., was pulled down about 1784 and a plain building of brick erected in its place. The high square pews were replaced by open seats in 1867; and in 1882 a new apsidal chancel was built and the church thoroughly repaired at a cost of £680. New Sunday Schools are also about to be built on a site kindly given by the Executors of the late Mr. E. Pease.

The monuments in the church bear the following inscriptions :—

Samuel Skey, Esq., of Spring Grove, Worcestershire, Lord of the Manor of Dowles, d. March 27, 1800, aged 74.

His whole life was one continued scene of Usefulness, Industry, and Benevolence, and few men have died more generally or more deservedly respected.

* See Dowles Parish Registers.

Also Sarah his wife, d. Dec. 5, 1790. Whose amiableness of disposition and goodness of heart endeared her to all who knew her.

Samuel Skey, of Spring Grove, only son of the above-named Samuel and Sarah Skey, d. 26 March, 1806, aged 47.

And of Samuel the eldest son of the last-named Samuel Skey and Sarah-Laurens his wife. He died 25th June, 1812, aged 10 years 9 months.

In the same vault are the remains of Sarah-Laurens, widow of the late Samuel Skey, and wife of Joseph Fletcher, A.M., Rector of this parish. On the 11th of July, 1840, in the 65th year of her age, she fell asleep in Christ Jesus.

Arthur the youngest and last surviving son of the above-named Samuel and Sarah Laurens Skey. Born Jan. 3, 1806, and died March 11th, 1860, aged 54.

Mary Burton, relict of William Burton, Esq., of Pollerton, Co. Carlow, Ireland, d. at Leamington Nov. 22nd, 1862, ætat. 70. "To me to live is Christ to die is gain."

Christopher Piggott Bancks, of the Heath, near Bewdley, born May 7, 1786, d. Feb. 21, 1865. His maxim was "To do justly love mercy and to walk humbly with his God."

Also of Christopher Whitcombe Bancks, the dearly loved only child of the above, born Aug. 21, 1849, d. April 20, 1856.

William Parsons, late of Bewdley. Some time a Senior Merchant in the service of the East India Company on their Establishment at Madrass. D. Aug. 18, 1816, aged 61.

Emma Prichard, d. 11 Nov., 1822, aged 73 years.

Edward Prichard, Esq., of Netherton, d. 22 Dec., 1851, aged 68.

Mary Prichard, wife of above, d. 14th July, 1860, aged 64.

Rev. Mr John Hassall, d. April 16, 1739, aged 56.

Mary his wife, d. Feb. 22, 1755, aged 65.

John their son, d. Sept. 3, 1764, aged 47.

James Hassall, late of Netherton, d. Jan. 23, 1794, aged 75.

"A family esteemed for their Honesty, Piety, Prudence, and Mutual Affection."

Elizabeth Howard, wife of the Rev. Thos. Howard, of Bewdley, and eldest dr. of Rev. Martin Crane, many years Rector of this parish. Ob. 12 July, 1757. Æ. 58.

Rev. Thomas Howard, 47 years Minister of Bewdley Chapel and 24 years Vicar of Neen Savage, in this county. Ob. 24 Sept., 1778. Æ. 72.

Joseph Crane, Alderman of Bewdley. Ob. 11 July, 1782. Æ. 73.

John Crane, Alderman of Bewdley, son of Thos. Crane, of Low Habberley, in the parish of Kidderminster, gent. Ob. 23 June, 1780. Æ. 42.

Thomas Howard Crane, of Bewdley, Esq., d. Nov. 4, 1852, aged 85. He was the senior member of the late Corporation of Bewdley.

Rev. Joseph Crane, of Bewdley, d. Sept. 9, 1860, aged 84.

Rev. John Cawood, M.A. Oxon, d. Nov. 7, 1852, aged 77.

James Cole, of Bewdley, Surgeon, d. Jan. 23, 1857, aged 70.

There is a memorial (1702) of several gifts for the poor of Dowles :—

> Thomas Grove : 1636 : 40*s.*
> Mr Walter Abbots Rector : 1683 : £2 10*s.*
> Humphrey Garmston : 1684 : 10*s.*
> Mr Nathaniel Williams Rector : 1701 : £5 for Bibles &c.
> Francis Radnal : 1703 : £2 10*s.*
> William Guy : 1706 : 10*s.*
> "The Righteous shall be in everlasting Remembrance."

All the above charities have long been lost.

Miss Ellen Vobe in 1840 left £100 to the poor, but it was not invested, and has all been distributed. She also left Dowles an interest in her gift of £500 for 12 "old maids."

The Rev. Joseph Crane and his two sisters each left £50 for the poor. This now brings in £4 7*s.* 6*d.* yearly.

Charles James Burton, Esq., of Richmond, by will dated 23rd of June, 1874, left £1000 for the poor not receiving alms or parochial relief. This produces £28 10*s.* yearly.

Mrs. Anne Prichard Smith, of Bridgnorth, in 1876 left £100 to the poor. This also is invested, and yields £2 18*s.* 6*d.* yearly.

In the churchyard is buried the body of William Pitt, an old soldier, who thus tells his story from a tombstone :—

> "At Dettingen and Fontenoy
> Death stared me in the face,
> But gave me furlough and convoy
> To meet him in this place."

William Le Grosvenor, who claimed to be the head of the family of the Grosvenors of Eaton Hall, is also buried in this churchyard.

In 1848 the hamlet of Button Oak, in the parish of Stottesdon, was transferred to Dowles for ecclesiastical purposes ; and an iron church was erected there in 1873 by the Rev. E. V. W. Davis, Rector.

The population of Dowles in 1881 was 127, and that of Button Oak 97.

Rectors of Dowles.*

Year	Date	Rector	Patron
1334	Apr. 14	John de Barnewell inst. to the Church of St. Lawrence of Dowles	Prior & Convent of Great Malvern
1368	Oct. 16	Henry de Ripple	Bp. *jur. dev.*
1385	Sept. 10	John Marsh	Prior & Conv.
1390	July 23	John Bulkere..	do.
1390	Dec. 2	Sir Edward Dabeneye ..	
1393	Aug. 20	Sir Philip de Hordeley ..	do.
1435	Aug. 19	Sir William Warewyke ..	do.
		Sir Thomas Dyer, ob. 1522..	do.
152$\frac{3}{4}$	Mar. 18	Sir William Talbot	Humphrey Woddall grantee *hac vice* of Prior & Convent
153$\frac{2}{3}$	Mar. 23	Sir John Gardiner, Dowles St. Andrew	Pr. & Conv.
		Thomas Blackwey	
1560	June 15	Henry Elston..	Bp. by lapse
1561	June 1	Ralphe Smythe	Do. *jure devol.*
157$\frac{0}{1}$	Mar. 13	Thomas Warter	Sir Geo. Blount, Kt., and Humph. Hill, gent.
		William Rogers, *sep.* Feb. 3, 1629..	
		Nathaniel Eston	
1661	Jul. 10	William Dalby	Francs Lord Newport
1669	Dec. 16	Walter Abbots	do.
1683		John Smeethes	Lord Herbert
1694	June 7	Nathaniel Williams.. ..	do.
1701	Jan. 27	William Price	do.
1707		Henry Baldwyn	do.
1710	Dec. 16	Martin Crane..	do.
1728		Butler Cowper	do.
1779		William Jesse	Henry Morley Herbert, Esq.
1814		Joseph Fletcher	
1871		Edward Valentine William Davis	
1876		John Richard Burton ..	Edward Pease, Esq.

* From the Blakeway MSS. in the Bodleian Library and from the Parish Registers.

Wribbenhall.

THIS name seems originally to have been given to a larger area than the present parish, and to have included Bewdley. The derivation of the word is uncertain, and it has been variously written as Gurbehale, Wrbehale, Wurbenhal', Wrobbenhale, Wurbenli, and Wrignall. The Bewdley side of old Wribbenhall was given in the 11th century to Worcester Monastery, but the present Wribbenhall, as a part of Kidderminster, seems to have remained in the hands of the Crown till Henry II. gave it to his Cupbearer, Manser de Biset. It remained in the hands of the Bisets till the reign of Edward I., when this family was represented only by two co-heiresses. One of them being afflicted with leprosy, gave her share to the Hospital for leprous women at Maiden Bradley, in Wiltshire. The other half, including Wribbenhall, belonged in 1337 to Sir Nicholas Burnell, and his son Sir Edward Burnell, of Acton Burnell, Salop, gave Eymore Wood in 8th King Edw. to the Priory of Worcester. After the dissolution of monasteries the wood was granted to the Dean and Chapter of Worcester; and the Ecclesiastical Commissioners, who now have the management of it, have lately recognized their responsibility as landlords by increasing the small endowment of the Vicarage. From the Burnells Wribbenhall came to the Barons of Abergavenny, and was purchased from them by Lord Foley, of Witley. In 1838 the hamlet passed into the hands of Lord Ward, now Earl of Dudley, who is the present lord of the manor.

Wribbenhall, from its excellent quays and vicinity to Bewdley, had formerly much commerce; and Brindley at first proposed making the basin of the canal here instead of at Stourport. At a spring tide as many as 400 pack horses have for several nights together been quartered in the place.*

In 1701 the chapel of "Christchurch in Wribbenhall" was built by subscription.† It was erected on a piece of garden ground held on lease by John Cheltenham under Lord Abergavenny, and a free sitting was to be allowed to Cheltenham. Afterwards the inhabitants deprived him of his seat, so by direction of Mr. Day, Lord Abergavenny's steward, the key was taken from the clerk and given to Cheltenham, who kept it, and let the clerk fetch it when he wished to toll the bell. Lord Abergavenny sold the estate to the Foleys; and in 1750 Lord Foley ordered Mr. Collins, the Curate, to deliver up the keys. He refused to do this without the consent of the inhabitants, so John Lewis (Lord Foley's steward) nailed up one door and put a padlock to the other. Mr. Boraston, Lord Foley's nominee, then attended and read prayers and homilies on Sundays. Before the Bishop's Court it was alleged that Lord Foley was sole proprietor of the *room* at Wribbenhall, and that if he wished he could pull it down or use it for any purpose he liked. The Attorney-General was, however, of opinion that Collins was curate for life, and that the inhabitants had a right in equity to the use of the chapel. The Register of Baptisms and Marriages begins April 8, 1723. The chapel was consecrated April 8, 1841, and the ground surrounding the chapel was at the same time consecrated as a burial-ground. In 1844 (June 19) a District Chapelry was assigned to the church, which thereupon became a Perpetual Curacy; and in 1856, under 19 and 20 Vic., c. 104, Wribbenhall was constituted a separate parish. The old church was well built, but completely devoid of architectural beauty; and in 1879 a new church was built dedicated to All Saints. The site had been given some years previously by the late Walter Chamberlain Hemming, Esq, and his widow contributed very largely to the building of

* *Nash*, Appendix, p. 47.

† Consecration sentence. Prattinton, however, says the chapel was built in 1719, and a new lease granted in 1728.

the new church. The old church was then pulled down, the disused churchyard enclosed, and a stone cross erected on the spot where the altar had stood.

There is a monumental brass in this church "In memory of Col. Philip Wodehouse, late of the 15th hussars, second son of the Rev. Philip Wodehouse, Prebendary of Norwich, born Aug. 6, 1788, died at Wribbenhall Dec. 11th, 1846. He was actively engaged during the war of the Revolution until he witnessed its termination on the field of Waterloo."

The beautiful east window was erected "To the Glory of God and in memory of Walter Chamberlain Hemming: died July 7, 1873."

Below another painted window is the following inscription :— "To the glory of God and in memory of an unselfish life. Martha daughter of the Rev. Edward Baugh: born 7 May, 1803; died Oct. 23, 1865."

In 1773 an advertisement in Berrows' *Worcester Journal* announced that Netherton Hall in this village was to be let. "There are Grates in the Fire-places, and the Rooms are genteelly hung with Paper."

Some Incumbents of Wribbenhall.

1720	Walter Jones
1722	John Hassall
1739	—— Bingham
1742	Daniel Collins
1749	——— Boraston
....	Thomas Wigan
....	Joseph Taylor
....	——— Miles
....	John Foley
....	—— Filewood
....	George Wharton, B.D.
1836	William Hallen
1850	Charles Warner
1864	Augustus William Gurney
1878	James Lamb Cheshire

Lower Areley.

OWER ARELEY or Areley Regis is about 3 miles below Bewdley. The church of St. Bartholomew is on a commanding situation overlooking the Severn Valley. From time immemorial Areley has been very closely connected with the larger parish of Martley. The lord of the manor of Martley was also lord of Areley; and the Rector of Martley still presents to the Rectory of Areley. In 3 Edw. I. John le Despencer was lord of the manor. Later on it came into the hands of the Mortimers, then of the barons Delaware, and from them by sale to the Mucklowes, who continued for many generations owners of Martley and Areley. In 1696 Thomas Zachary, Esq., married Elizabeth Mucklowe, and in 1766 the manor passed by descent to their grandson Thomas Zachary, and from him to the present owner, Sampson Zachary Lloyd, Esq.

Areley Hall is an ancient manor house, and Prince Rupert is said to have slept in it before the battle of Worcester. Mr. Lloyd has an extensive collection of deeds from the time of Henry III. downwards, and also an interesting MS. containing the Household Expenses of Simon Mucklowe, who lived in the reign of James I.

The chief object of curiosity in Areley churchyard is a wall about 18 or 20 feet in length built up of eight large sandstone blocks, each stone being more than 4 feet long and about 1½ ft. square. On it is the inscription—

"*Λιθολογημα Quare*
Repenitur Sir Harry."

For a long time there was great speculation as to who "Sir Harry" might be. The registers were lost and there was no other record. But (as showing the value of internal evidence)

Sir Harry's tomb : Areley-Kings

in Astley church is a monument to the Rev. Thomas Bowater, Rector of Astley.

"His soul Heaven has
Dirt dirt does cover
Our Saviour saw one such,
We one other;
Of his successors shall be said hereafter
As good or bad, as like, unlike Bowater."
Signed—" Henricus Coningsby, Eques auratus, 1696."

It was argued (and as it turned out justly) that in an illiterate age there could not be two rhyming "Sir Harry's," and hence the Λιθολογημα was conjecturally assigned to be Sir Henry Coningsby's tomb. This proved correct, for in 1842 a perfect copy of the Areley Kings' burial registers was found in a lumber room at Tewkesbury, and in it occurs the entry "the 8th day of December, 1701, Sir Harry Consby, Knight, was buried in wollin, according to ye late act of Parl^t^."

This Knight was an ancestor of the Earls of Essex, and lived at Hampton Court, Herefordshire, where he dropped accidentally his only child into the moat, and was so afflicted by the loss that he retired as a recluse to a small property called The Sturt, Areley, whence he superintended the erection of his monument as a permanent *pané* or portion of the churchyard fence, while the other *panés* being formed of wood have long since disappeared. Sir H.Coningsby also planted three walnut trees near the slab covering his remains at the foot of the above dwarf wall; and made a bequest in his will that the boys of the parish were to crack the nuts on the said slab on a certain day in the year. But in the long Revolutionary War (1790—1815) walnut wood was valuable for gunstocks, and the trees were felled, and the boys deprived of their sports. The wall of blocks is now much distorted, and the sandstone is so friable that ere many years are past only a heap of sandy dust will be left. Sir Harry Coningsby was a descendant of Thomas Coningsby, who died in 1498 and was buried in Rock church.

In the chancel is an inscription to the memory of Walter Walsh, who died in 1702. It records that he was "ruinated by three Quackers, two lawyers, and a fanatick to help them."

To many the chief interest in Areley Regis will arise from the fact that it was the residence of Layamon, the author of the "Brut," one of the earliest books written in the English tongue. Mr.J.R.Green says, "Historically it is worthless, but as a monument of our language it is beyond all price. After Norman and Angevin English remained unchanged. In more than thirty thousand lines less than fifty Norman words are to be found."* There are two MSS. of Layamon's "Brut," the one written early in the 13th century, the other about half a century later. The earlier version is in the *Southern* dialect, while the later has many *Midland* peculiarities. Both texts were edited by Sir Frederick Madden in 1847, from the Cottonian MSS. for the Society of Antiquaries.† It is much to be desired that some memorial of Layamon should be placed in his church. Mrs. Baldwyn Childe has designed and erected a beautiful window to the memory of another great early English writer, William Longland (Piers the Ploughman), in Cleobury church, Shropshire? Will no one in Worcestershire do the same for this equally distinguished writer of his county?

* Green's *Short History of the English People*, p. 117.
† Morris' *Specimens of Early English Text*, p. 64.

Rectors of Areley Kings.

Patrons.	Incumbents.
	Layamon son of Leovenath, *c.* 1200
	Johannes de le Ryvere, ... 1282
Johannes de Chausy, Rector de Martley	Henricus Everard, cap. 14 kal. Jul., 1311
	Ricardus Fillob, cap. 10 kal. Dec. 1323
David Maynard, Rector de Martley..	Johannes le Clere, pbr. 9 Sept. ....
Johannes Savsy do. ..	Will'us de Ideshale, 20 Sept., 1354
Will'us de Hulle do. ..	Will'us Flayting, 16 Jan., 1363
W. Brugge, R...	Will'us atte More, 11 Sept., 1369
W. Reede, R.	Thomas Cross, 1401
	Joh. Wybbe, 8 Dec., 1404
	Richardus Cone, 23 Oct., 1405
Thomas Pontesbury, R.	Thomas Cross, 22 Oct., 1407
	Ricardus Sodden, 4 Nov., 1416
R. de Marteley..	Thomas Frensche, 19 Jan., 1419
John Greve, R...	Johannes Richard, 17 Jun., 1454
	Johannes Maryten, 8 Oct., 1458
	Ricardus Richards, Nov., 1464
Will'us Feld, R.	Walterus John, 25 Jan., 1472
Joh. Paul, R.	Ricardus Oldenale, 22 Oct., 1479
R. de Martley	Johannes Wall, 1 Nov., 1485
Walt. Baker, R.	Ricardus Bogy, 11 Jan., 1509
	Will'us Wartry, 23 Nov., 1520
Rogerus Walker, R.	Will'us Weston, 25 Oct., 1558
Fr. Jones, R.	John James, 3 May, 1577
	Humphrey Walker, 7 May, 1589
Rob. Wylde of Worcester, by grant of John Vernon	John Vernon, 8 Aug., 1682
Rob. Vernon	Richard Vernon, 4 Oct., 1710
R. of Martley	John Haughton, 1 Oct., 1733
	Thomas Vernon, 29 May, 1738
Thos. Dunne, R. of Martley.. ..	George Hulme, 1794
The Lord Chancellor (for this turn).	Henry James Hastings, Oct., 1831
H. J. Hastings, R. of Martley ..	John Parsons Hastings, July, 1856
J. P. Hastings, R. of Martley ..	Edward Acton Davies, Oct., 1875
Ditto	Daniel Vawdrey, Sept., 1880

Upper Arley.

RLEY, anciently written Earnley, means "an open place in a wood, the abode of the Eagle."* An osprey or sea eagle was shot there in the present century by Lord Valentia's keeper.† In 996 Arley was given by Wulfruna, widow of Aldhelm Earl of Northampton, to a religious house at Wolverhampton (Wulvrune's Hampton). In the time of William II. Bishop Sampson diverted Arley to Worcester Priory. Bishop Roger (*temp.* Henry I.) gave it to a Judge, Henry de Port, who built and endowed the church. Adam de Port, his son, placed the living in the hands of the Bishop of Lichfield. Later on Hubert de Burgh sold to Robert de Glovernia "certain lands in the Ville of Arley," which had been the lands of Osbert de Hextan. In the church is a stone figure in armour with crossed legs, and bearing a shield *three bars dencetté gules.* Bishop Lyttelton supposed that the knight was a de Hextan. The Rev. E. Hardwicke surmised that he was Sir Richard Delamare. The late Rev. Mackenzie Walcott believed him to be Walter de Balun, who married Isolda, daughter of Edmund de Mortimer and heiress of Upper Arley (*Nash*, vol. ii., app. iv.). A sketch of the tomb is given opposite page 72, but the knight's identity is still uncertain.

Richard Duke of York sold this manor to Sir William Burley, of Broncroft Castle. Burley had two daughters, one of whom, Joan, married the famous Judge Sir Thomas Lyttelton; and

---

* *Aar* is the German for eagle, and the *erne* is the "bog-eagle" of Scotland.

† *Analyst*, No. ii., p. 84, Sept., 1834.

thus the manor was carried to the Lytteltons, who enjoyed it for 300 years. From 1650 Arley was the chief seat of this distinguished family, and many of their monuments are still in the church. When George the "good" Lord Lyttelton built Hagley Hall, Arley fell into the background. Thomas the "bad" Lord Lyttelton left Arley to his sister's son, George Viscount Valentia and 2nd Earl of Mountnorris. The fine castle at Arley was built by Lord Mountnorris on the site of the old manor house; and, together with the church, forms a striking feature in the landscape. The castle grounds contain many specimens of rare trees, one of especial interest being the Sorb Tree,* the largest now in England. The Earl died in 1844 without issue; and soon afterwards the estate was purchased by Robert Woodward, Esq., whose eldest son succeeded him as lord of the manor in 1882. The parish registers commence in 1564. The following is an imperfect list of

RECTORS OF UPPER ARLEY.

	Incumbents.		Patrons.
Temp. Henry III.	Philip de Bray	..	Bp. of Lichfield
1632—1655	John Thomas	..	
.... 1662	—— Orford	..	
.... 1684	John Waldron.. ..	..	
1684—1707	Thomas Parkes ..	..	
1707—1758	Joseph Chellingworth	..	
1758—1794	John Brooke	..	George, Lord Lyttelton
1794—1800	Thomas Simon Butt..	..	George, Viscount Valentia
1800	Thomas Butt	..	Ditto
1851—1862	Richard Hart Ingram	..	
1862	Charles James Wilding	..	

* See *Miscellanea.*

The Rock *or* Aka.

HESE two names, seemingly so different, according to Bishop Percy, are identical. The village was called Aca or "The Oak" in Latin, and the English "The Rock," is only a corruption of the old Anglo-Saxon Thær Ac, that is Ther Oak, or The Oak. Dr. Percy believed firmly in the tradition that the original Oak, which thus gave its name to the parish, was the same where St. Augustine had the famous interview with the British Bishops, as narrated by the Venerable Bede. "In the meantime, Augustine, with the assistance of King Ethelbert, drew together to a conference the bishops or doctors of the next province of the Britons, at a place which is to this day called Augustine's Ac, that is Augustine's Oak, on the borders of the Wiccii and the West Saxons."* In an old atlas preserved at Shakenhurst, entitled "The large English Atlas, By Emanuel Bowen, Printed by John Bowles at the Black Horse in Cornhill"—presumably of the date A.D. 1670—Rocke is mentioned as noted for Augustine's oak, where he and the British clergy held a Conference.

Bishop Percy says, "When the new Turnpike Road was first made [1753] the Gate being set up at the Apostle's Oak, the Gatekeeper, till his House was built, took shelter in the old hollow Trunk, in which he made a fire that caused it to be

---

* *Ven. Bædæ Hist. Eccles.*, lib. II. cap. ii.

burnt down. I remember being told this by Mr. Meysey Rector of the Rock about the year 1754 or 1755 when I was on a Visit at his Parsonage house."*

In Saxon times Godric and Alward, thanes of Earl Algar, held respectively the hamlets of Alton and Lindon. Ulmer held Halac and Grim owned More. In the Conqueror's time it was the land of Ralph de Tony, and was afterwards held under him by the Abbot and Convent of St. Ebrulph at Utica in Normandy. Later on Rock and Snede were owned by Henry de Ribbesford, and afterwards came to Beauchamp Earl of Warwick. By attainder 15th Hen. VII. the manor fell to the Crown, and was granted 37 Hen. VIII. to Richard Andrews, who alienated Roke and Sued to Robert Acton. Alton and Roke were granted 1 Eliz. to George Blount by Bryan Carter and Mary his wife. John Coningsby had lands in Roke and Sued by lease from the king: these descended to Fitzwilliam Coningsby of the Bower.

The church is dedicated to St. Peter, and part of it is of Norman work, notably the fine chancel arch. The chancel deviates slightly to the south—a symbol of the leaning of our Saviour's head upon the Cross. The tower was erected in 1510 by Judge Coningsby, who also built the chantry of St. Mary and St. George, in which is his altar tomb. The incised effigy of Richard Smythe, Rector of the church (1529—1554), in his vestments, is now let in the wall of the chantry. The church was thoroughly restored about 20 years ago by the Rev. Arthur Severne.

The chapel of St. Giles at Heightington in this parish is also of great antiquity, and the interior was once adorned with fresco paintings and stained glass.

Richard Baxter says that in his time there were two curates of Rock: one got his living by tying faggots, the other by making rope.

* From an autograph letter to Robert Bromley, Esq., of Abberley Lodge, now in the possession of Miss Bromley, of Bewdley. The letter is headed "Near Northampton, May 31, 1797."

RECTORS OF ROCK.

PATRONS.	INCUMBENTS.
Pope John	Peter de Hope, 5 kal. Oct., 1333
King	Richard le Clerke, 9 Oct., 1338
	Roger de Stanford, 11 Sept., 1340
Abbot and Convent of St. Ebrulph in Normandy	John de Friseby, 16 Dec., 1361
King	Richard Attewell, 16 May, 1381
	William Kydermynster, 28 Oct., 1385
	Richard Crateford, 4 Feb., 1385
Robert, Prior of Mountgrace ..	Thomas Ewyer, 21 May, 1398
Bishop	William Lamprey, 31 Aug., 1399
King	Roland Blund, 14 Apr., 1414
	Robert Skinner, *alias* Montgomery, 13 Apr., 1415
Prior and Convent of Shene.. ..	William Coryngham, 1 June, 1416
	John Thedilthorp, 1 Nov., 1426
	John Wyllys, 12 June, 1439
	John Spencer, 10 Decem., 1481
	John Algar, 17 Nov., 1514
	Richard Smyth, 3 March, 1529
Thomas Grene, by grant from the Convent of Shene (?)	John Cuthbert, 26 April, 1560
	Thomas Hopkins, 1 Aug., 1565
	William Coke (or Cooke), d. 1607
	——— Benson, D.D., 1607
Edward Boyleston	Sares Boyleston, 4 Nov., 1672
	Edward Partington, 13 July, 1716
John Meysey	William Petwin, 24 Sept., 1731
	John Meysey, 9 March, 1732
Francis Watkins	Ralph Lingen, 16 Oct., 1764
Charles Watkins Meysey	Richard Watkins, 11 Aug., 1770
	Ralph Lingen
	William Henry Hill, 1812
John Michael Severne	William Severne, 1840
Anna Maria Severne	Arthur Severne, 1853
Alfred James	Alfred James, 1862
Caroline Reiss	Frederick Augustus Reiss, 1870

The church of the Holy Trinity in the Far Forest was consecrated in 1844. The parish was taken out of Rock and Ribbesford, and the patronage is alternately in the gift of the Rectors of those parishes. The Registers date from 1848, and appended is a

LIST OF INCUMBENTS OF THE FAR FOREST.

Robert Onebye Walker ..	1844—1848	Rector of Ribbesford
James T. C. Saunders	1848—1853	Rector of Rock
Josiah Turner Lea	1853	Rector of Ribbesford

Lower Mitton.

OWER MITTON (Stourport) is mentioned in Domesday as one of the hamlets of Kidderminster under the name of *Metune*. John Cofton, of Cofton Hacket, was anciently seized of lands here, which descended to his heiress, Lucy wife Alex. de Hodington, 20 Edw. III. (1245), and in this line it continued till 7 Henry VI. John Lench, a Lancastrian, forfeited it by his attainder in 3 Edw. IV., but Henry VII. restored his son, John Lench, to this his paternal estate. Afterwards Sir William Lygon held it, but sold to every tenant the inheritance of the estate he occupied. Later on he sold the manor to James Clent. In 1563 Mitton chapelry contained 23 families.

There has been a chapel at Mitton for centuries, but burials used to be made at Kidderminster. In 1625 (Nov. 13) the ground lying round the chapel was consecrated for burials by John, Bishop of Worcester. Mr. John Odell, Vicar of Kidderminster, John Yarranton and John Wilkes, chapelwardens of Mitton, and John and Humphrey Grove, gentlemen there, were the petitioners. The Vicar of Kidderminster and his successors were to receive for the burial of every person in the churchyard 6*d*., for a burial in the chapel 6*s*. 8*d*., and in the chancel 10*s*.*

The present plain brick church of *St. Michael* was erected on the old site in 1791. In 1844 (June 19) the hamlet of Lower Mitton was made a chapelry district, and the chaplain became a perpetual curate. In 1866 (Aug. 7), by Lord Blandford's Act, the curacy became a vicarage, and the present incumbent is the first vicar. The earliest register is dated 1693; and the patron has always been the Vicar of Kidderminster.

The foundations of a new church from the designs of Sir Gilbert Scott were begun on Sept. 8, 1881, and were completed last year. About £4000 have been promised or paid to the new church fund; and it is believed that £8000 more would complete the nave, so as to make it available for divine service.

---

* The deed is printed in *Nash*, vol. ii., p. 59.

The hamlet of Upper Mitton (in Hartlebury) has been lately attached to Lower Mitton; and the new church of All Saints there has been erected at the sole cost of Alfred Baldwin, Esq., of Wilden House.

The visits of John Wesley to Stourport have already been mentioned (page 50).

"About 1766, where the river Stour empties itself into the Severn below Mitton, stood a little alehouse called Stourmouth. Near this Brindley has caused a town to be erected, made a port and dockyards, built a new and elegant bridge,* established markets, and made it the wonder not only of this county but of the nation at large. In the year 1795 it consisted of 250 houses and about 1300 inhabitants. Thus was the sandy barren common at Stourport converted, in the space of 30 years, into a flourishing, healthy, and very populous village."†

Acts of Parliament for the construction of the Worcestershire and Staffordshire Canal were passed in 1765 and 1770, and the principal basin was made at Stourport. The canal is 46 miles in length, and has 44 locks: the total cost of construction was £105,000.

By the Reform Act, Stourport was joined to the Parliamentary borough of Bewdley. The list of members is given in the Appendix (page xl.).

Stourport is still a thriving town, and carries on the manufacture of carpets, iron and tin wares, leather, screws, and barges.

Appended is a list of some

INCUMBENTS OF MITTON CHAPEL.

1552	W. Spytull	1779	John Grubb
1663	Timothy Kirk	1781	Francis Baines
1669	Edward Thomas	1782	David Davies
1671	John Brown	1829	Charles Wharton
1692	Nathaniel Williams	1850	Stephen Richard Waller
1694	Jonathan Cotton	1861	Benjamin Gibbons

* The bridge erected in 1775 was destroyed by a flood in 1794, and an iron bridge of one arch, 150 feet span, was set up in its place. This bridge was rebuilt in 1870.

† *Nash*, appendix p. 47.

APPENDIX.

Extracts from Ribbesford Church Registers.

In the year of our lord god 1598. + FINS

This Regester Booke was copped owte by awarde made at the Parlement houlden at Westmenster in the forteyeth year of the Raigne of o[r] Soverane Lady Elizabethe By the Grace of god Queene of England, ffraunce & Irelond Defender of the faythe.

The entries from 1574 to 1598 were copied "from an oulde booke"—part of which was missing—"by John Glover, Clk. of p'sh."

Georgius Sowthall Artium Baccalaureus Concionator publicus inductus fuit Rector de Ribbesford decimo septimo die Januarii Anno Dni. millesimo sexcentesimo.

BAPTISMS.

1574	Dec.	12.	John the sonne of Ambros Hartley, Caper
	Feb.	3.	Margret the daughter of a Litell taylor.
1575	Aprell	1.	Annes the Daughter of thomas warter,* Clarke
	Nov.	27.	Elizabethe the daughter of John Grove, hatter
	Jan.	26.	John the sonn of M[r] Anthony mucklow †
	Feb.	20.	Robarte the sonn of John Vickres
			Be mercifull unto us God of thy godnes
1576	Sept.	9.	John the sonn of william holms, sherman
	Sept.	21.	ffraunces the sonne of John Bolton, taner
	Nov.	27.	william the sonn of Humffrey unckels
			Call to Remembrance thy sinns and offences.
1577	Nov.	1.	Joane the daughter of humffrey Brasher

* Chaplain of St. Andrew's, Bewdley, and Rector of Dowles.

† Son of Richard Mucklowe, Esq., of Hodon.

Delle with the thinge that Lawful and Righte for so shall hit ples god beter then sacrefesses of Bullockes and yonge shee asses

1577 Jan. 4. Thomas the sonn of thomas warter minyster
1578 May 17. Richard the son of Richard Jones the curat of Ripsford

End dewer thou unto the end thowghe thou suffer greate Trubles and Extremicties for the trewthe sake

1580 Katheren the daughter of John Glover* shewmaker
1580 Nov. 20. Thomas the son of thomas Bowlson †
1581 Ap. 13. Josnath the sonn of Humfrey Brasher
Ap. 20. Robart the son of Robarte Acton Esquier ‡
Feb. 27. moyses beinge fownd in a owt hows
1582 Aug. 28. John the sonn of ffraunces hill, taner
March 3. Philipe the sonn of Harry Grove goner
1583 Oct. 10. Richard the sonn of Rowland Longley p'son of Corle §
1584 Feb. 7. ffortune the daughter of Mr Robart Acton Esquier
Feb. 24. John the sonn of Richard Brian flecher ‖
1585 May 30. Edward the sonne of Nickolas Crondall Clark
1586 July 11. John the sonne of John Hayles tanner
Sept. 24. John the sonne of Richard townesend a straynger
1588 Aug. 11. Arculus the daughter of Edward Bayles
Sept. 22. George the sonne of Henry Hathweye Lp farryer
1589 Ap. 13. Elenor the daughter of olever thloyd ¶
1590 Ap. 1. Anne the daughter of Thomas morres a glover
July 13. Margret the daughter of a straynger came to the Councell
1592 March 26. Henry the sonne of John Sowley tanner
Aug. 9. ffraunces the sonne of Edward Robinson a Bower
1593 Oct. 14. Katheren the daughter of John Wilkes
Nov. 15. Sibell the daughter of John Hayley
March 16. Edward the sonne of Edward Plevey
1594 Sept. 17. Isabell the daughter of John Pardoe
Oct. 30. Anne the daughter of thomas Dedicott of wrignall
1596 Oct. 28. Thomas the sonne of Thomas Goughe parchment maker
1597 Jan. 13. Peregrine the sonn of Richard franklen the usher

GOD *save Elizabethe our Queene. Amen.*

BURIALLS.

1575 Dec. 26. Ann the dawghter of Mr Henry Blonte Esquier from horshill
Jan. 4. mistres Blonte the wiffe of Mr Henry Blont Esquer

* The parish clerk who copied this Register, and inserted the religious and moral maxims in the margin.
† First Bayliff of Bewdley, 1606. ‡ Owner of Ribbesford.
§ Coreley (?) ‖ Maker of arrows.
¶ The Welsh pronunciation of "Lloyd." Dr. Beddoe, F.R.S., of the Anthropological Society, says that the people of Bewdley still have much of the Celtic or Celtiberian physical type, their hair particularly being more often dark than that of their neighbours east of the Severn.

1576 Feb. 24. Margret the dawghter of David verrett *
1577 March 19. A stranger ladd was buried
1580 Nov. 21. Elenor taylor a owld wenche
March 8. Anne Knyghte a prisnor owt of the Jayle of woster
1582 Feb. 4. William the sonne of Philipe Turstone Clarke
1585 June 27. Owen Apprichard

ther was Buried in this year 1587 of a straynge sicknes in this p'ishe of Ripsford 84.

1588 Ap. 21. owlde mother Kidder widdow
July 6. william mathewes a Clarke of the Councell
1589 July 7. Master John Drap Debetey of Bewdley
1590 July 8. A welchwoman that came to the Councell
1592 Jan. 13. Sister a poor wench a strayngere

1593 [Burials in June 4, in July 11, in Aug. 50, in Sept. 45, in Oct. 27, in Nov. 18, in Dec. 11. Total for the year 202.]

Aug. 1. Mr Thomas warter minester of Bewdley
" 6. Thomas the sonne of John ap Bowen
" 16. Robarte the sonne of John ap Bowen
" 17. John ap Bowen Capper
" 17. Annes Bowen his wiffe
" 17. Ales the dawghter of the sayd John ap Bowen
" 17. Richard the sonne of the sayd John ap Bowen
" 18. Ales the dawghter of Henry James
" 21. The sonne of Henry James
" 21. The dawghter of Harye James
" 24. The dawghter of Harye James
" 24. Th'other dawghter of Henry James
Sept. 14. Alles James
" 15. Henry James

Geve no occasion of Evell But fear gods Anger
The Lord take us to his mercye amen.

[The total number of deaths in 1594 was only 44.]

Prayse God allways.

1596 Dec. 22. Richard the father of John Vickreg of the age on 100 yeares and 1 yeare departed at myten
Feb. 25. John Myllard of glathermyll
1598 July 24. ther was buryead the harte and Bowels of Mr Sherrer †
Aug. 1. George Leathe of wrignall was drownded as he was goinge to wesh himself in Severn in a storme of Littinge and thunder on Lamas Even at nyghte

* Arms formerly in S. window of Ribbesford Church.

† Thos. Sherer, Esq., Clerk to the Council of the Marches: his body was buried at Shrewsbury, of which town he was Bailiff in 1589.

MATRIMONY Anno Dni 1574.

1597	July	10.	Thomas Stiche and Indians his wiffe.
	Dec.	30.	George Sowthall Parson of Ribbesford and Bridgett Stookes were married att worcester.
1604	Oct.	8.	Richard Whittcott and Margarett Sowley att dowlls in licentia
1609	Oct.	30.	William Hopkyns * and Hellen Vickaris
1613	Apr.	21.	ffraunces Gildinge † and Issabel Beste
1615	Maye	24.	Thomas Hill & ffraunces Shelly at dowles
	Oct.	12.	Arthyr Palmer & Elizabeth Shelly at dowles
1618	June	1.	Silvanus Sare & Joyce Tombes
1640	Feb.	9.	Nicolas Kendricke and Ann Phillips
1647	Dec.	27.	Thomas Wright Rector of Hartlebury & Joyce Pountney vid.
1652	Ap.	19.	Walter Pallmer & Anne Clare

BENEFACTORS TO RIBSFORD AND BEWDLEY.

Anno Dni 1633

In the yeare above written Sir Henry Herbert, Knight, Patron of the Church and Lord of the mannor of Ribsford, bestowed upon the said Church the great greene Cushion whereof the upper p[t] is velvet & the lower p[t] Sattin, together with the case of greene shagg-bayes to keepe, carry, and preserve it in, the cushion to be for the pulpitt when sermons are therein delivered: which cushion was stollen, and one like it bought and p[d] for by the

Anno Dni 1634

In this yeare the same Sir Henry Herbert Knight bestowed also upon the Church of Ribsford a carpett of greene broad-cloath with a greene silk fringe about it to be put upon the Communion Table: and also did line and studd the desk of the pulpit in the said Church.

Anno Dni 1636

In this yeare Mrs. Margarett Whitcott ‡ wid: gave (for a new yeare's gift) unto the Church of Ribsford a Communion Cupp of Silver with a Cover for the same, weighing seventeen ounces tearmeing it the widowes mite. The same yeare the above-mentioned Sir Henry Herbert Knight gave unto the Church of Ribsford also a large Communion Cupp of silver with a cover for the same weighing . . . ounces, with case to preserve it in with this inscription§

* "The most eminent wise and truly religious magistrate of Bewdley, at last Member of the Long Parliament."—Richard Baxter. See Burials, July, 1647.

† One of the donors of the Mill and Meadow Money.

‡ *Née* Soley. See "Registers," Oct. 8, 1604.

§ Inscription on silver cup:—

Soli Deo Gloria

Poculum benedictionis cui benedicimus nonne communio Sanguinis Christi est Cap x Pauli ad Corinth. Donum Henrici Herberti Eq. Ecclesiæ de Ribsford Anno Dom 1636 mens. mart. Ante Festum Paschæ.

Anno Dni 1637

In this yeare Richard Vickris merchant and then cheife Sheriffe of the Citie of Bristol gave a greene Cushion of Plush to be used upon the pulpit in the Chappell of Bewdley.

Anno Dni 1638

In this yeare against Easter the same most liberall and worthy Benefactor Sir Henry Herbert gave to the Church of Ribsford a silver flagon for the wine at times of administration of the Sacrament of the Lord's Supper weighing . . . with a case to preserve it in.

In the same yeare the said Sir Henry Herbert also was at the care & cost of making that cupp which Mrs. Whitcott (aforenamed) gave, and a little old one which the Church had formerly belonging to it, into one, proportionable and uniform with the great cupp of his gift abovementioned with a cover of silver thereunto; for wh Cup and cover he gave also a case for the safe keeping and preservation. All which he hath freely done, given & bestowed to the glory of God, the ornament of the Church, and the exemplarie encouragement of others.

Anno Dni 1639

In this yeare also against Easter the abovesaid worthy Knight Sir Henry Herbert gave to the Church of Ribsford another silver flagon followeing the first, for the same use as is abovementioned weighing . . . with a case to preserve it in.* The same Sir Hen. Herbert gave 4 pewter potts with hanglesses to carry them by, to containe the wine at the communion.

BAPTISMS.

1604 March 10. Elizabethe the daughter of Richard Inett tanner on the wyre hill

1615 May 29. Thomas the Sonn of Thomas Paramore Gente of Ripsford was baptised the viijth Daye of June & was borne xxix Daye of Maye.

A true Coppye of a Letter sent from the Worpll William Sebright to the worpll the Bayliffe, the Parson, the Corporation of the Towne of Bewdley, & the p'ishioners of the p'ish of Ribsford. [He gives 56*s*. 4*d*. yearly to provide "against every Sabaoth day for ever hereafter, the quantity of thirteene pennyworth of good sweete and holesome bread of wheate, the same to be set uppon the Communion Table at the beginning of morning prayer."]

Copy of part of the last will of Mr Samuell Sayer of Needlestead in the County of Suffolke Esquier, 1623. [He provides Almshouses for 6 poor men & endows them with £5 each.]

* The inscription on this flagon is :—

Implete & haurite nunc
Hoc est novum illud pactum
per meum Sanguinem
Donum etc. 1639.

Mem. that Sir Henry Herbert in 1633 bestowed the greate greene Cushion wherof the upper part is Velvet & the lower part Sattin for the use of Ribsford Church at any time of preaching in the said church, or upon especiall occasion (now & then happening) for the like use of the Chappell in Bewdley.

1624 Nov. 2. Thomas sonne of Willm Madstard * & Alice

Nov. 25. Charles sonne of the Right Honourable Spencer Lord Cumpton beinge baptized in the Chappell of ye Mannour house called Ticknell, & borne on ye 24th day of October †

1626 July 30. William the sonne of William Tither ‡ and Anne

1630 Aug. 15. Elizabeth ye daughter of Anne Lambert supposed to be the daughter of a stranger whose name to ye said Anne was unknown as she sayth upon examination

1634 Manoah the sonne of Manoah Sherrard High Schoolemaster & Elizabeth

1637 July 30. Richard ye Sonne of Robert Morton Minister

1639 Sept. 8. Sares § the sonne of Thomas Boilston & Anne

BURIALS.

1599 Dec. 17. A poore boy out of the Queen's stable

1601 Francis Corbet of the Park myll

1603 Sept. 17. Susanna the daughter of John Morgan *the peste*

1604 Oct. 10. Sara Barnsley out of the cabbin ¶ *the peste.*

[From Oct. 1604 to April 1605 there were 115 deaths from the peste or plague, of whom 23 belonged to the family of Barnsley]

1607 Nov. 25. Mrs Elizabeth Churchill wife of Mr John Churchill Esquire of Ribbesford dyed at London on St Stephen's day Anno Dom. 1606

1608 Ap. 25. Gabriell Brasier of Burford who was slaine on St George's day

1609 May 27. John weaver the Baker of the george over agaynst the Chappell

1610 David Taylor alias Pint pott

1611 Mr John Grove gent sometimes Deputy of Bewdley

May 7. Lewis Morris Minister of the Chappell being Curatt there

1613 Mr Andrewe Armstronge—a Scottish gentleman killed at Kinlet and brought to Ribbesford and buried there. He was killed on the 13th, and buried on the 15th, April

1614 March 23. Clemen Vaughan the wife of meredethe vaughan did drowne herself in the parke pooll at the myll.

* Chaplain of Bewdley.
† Grandson of William Earl of Northampton.
‡ This is still the local pronunciation of "Tudor."
§ Afterwards minister of Bewdley and Rector of Rock.
¶ See Chapel Wardens' Accounts.

1616 a crisom child * of Robert Slater

1621 Oct. 17. Thomas Boylson gent. the first Bayliffe of Bewdley

1623 May 24. Richard Gardiner a stranger, servant to the Earl of Northampton the then Lord President of Wales

William Arnold a stranger who was drowned in the well in the upper Street

William Perrott (sonne of Mr Humphrey Perrott of Bel-hall) who was slaine in Bewdley †

1626 Mr John Tyler one of ye capitall Burgesses

1632 Oct. 5. Francis the sonne of Thomas Allen of Great Hedgwicke was buried at Ribsford beinge scalded to death & searched by a Jury in Bewdley the Bayliffe being Coroner

1635 June 20. Elizabeth ye wife of Robert Swath at Cleobury beinge excommunicated in Ribsford her owne p'ish

Feb. 25. Alice ye wife of Edmound Bishopp of greate Hedgwicke was buryed by night at Cleobury

1636 Jan. 31. Edmund Bishopp of greate hedgwick was buryed at Cleobury Mortimer by Richard Osland then Deacon there havinge stood excom. in the church of Ribsford for many years

1637 Jan. 9. Thomas Corbett gente. the peste

1641 Anne Steward who was killed with a fall into a well at ye widow Greaves—hir house

1643 Mr Thomas Hincksman of London was buryed there; who dyed the 8th day of Nov., and had a funerall sermon preached at Bewdley in remembrance of him, and a funerall dinner kept Decemb. 12

1645 March 26. John Hams and John Hobs, soldiers

„ 30. Andrew Coltis, a souldier

Aug. 13. Thomas Gossage & Thomas Haszald, souldiers

„ 14. Lieutenant Smelling, souldier

[In 1645-6 there were 21 burials of "souldiers."]

1647 July 21. William Hopkins gent. a gracious & able Christian; then Burgesse elected for parliament for the Burrough of Bewdley died 19

[In 1648 the "peste" carried off about 60 persons.]

1652 Feb. 21. Mr John Solie dyed at Dowles 17th

[In 1652 the entries give day of death as well as of burial. Many were buried on the day of their death: very few later than the next day. Only winding sheets were used—rarely coffins. See "Chapel Wardens' Accounts" in Appendix.]

---

* See Shakspere's *Henry V.*, Act ii. sc. 3.

† See *Midland Antiquary*, vol. i, p. 117, for an account of the Perrott family.

VOLUME II.

At the hundred house the 23rd Sept. 1633 before Edward Pytts, William Jeffreys, & John Lathum Esqrs & Justices of the peace for the County of Worcester

Whereas it appeareth unto us upon a Certificate delivered unto us from the p'ishioners & Inhabitants of the p'ish of Ribsford that they have made choice of Mr John Boraston to be Register for the sayd p'ish wee the sayd Justices do hereby approve & allow of the sayd John Boraston to have the keeping of this Register book according to an Act of Parliamt passed the 24th of Aug. 1653. And we have sworne him to execute the sayd Office dilligently & faithfully according to the sayd Act.

[120 births in 1657: 100 in 1658: 101 in 1659: 120 in 1660.]

BAPTISMS.

1657 Feb. 15. Leonard son of Leonard Simpson Esq * & Elizabeth

1663 Bap. Feb. 9 Richard, † son of William Willis & Susanna borne January 17

1668 July 3. Mabell, d. of Hughe Yarranton & Margery

" 3. Jonathan, s. of Hughe Yarranton & Margery

" 3. Penelope, d. of Hughe Yarranton & Margery

This last was borne June 18, the age of ye other two was of Mabell about 4 yeares, & of Jonathan about 2 yeares

Hughe & Margery—(if not maryed) were presented for ffornication before marriage (if yet maryed) & excommunicated, & kept the two first so long unbaptized, but having a 3rd. were all three baptized together.

1671 Feb. 9. Thomas son of Thomas ffarloe & Joane. borne in Aprill 1665. baptized before by a minister not ordain'd by a Byshop, for wch his ffather was p'sented & ordered to have this child baptized by one episcopally ordained

1671 Oct. 2. Susanna‡ d. of Obadiah Wowen & Susanna, borne Sept. 11

March 12. {Partington, Thomas} twin sons of Mr Sares Bolston & Anne, borne ffeb. 23

1718 Sept. 30. Elizabeth dr of Jonn Soley junr of Samburn in ye Parish of Kidderminster gent. & Elizabeth. Baptised at Samburn by Dr Stillingfleet

1719 Feb. 12. A daughter of John Bedford & Judith (Anabaptists) whom they call Esther born Feb. 5

1720 March William Dugard of the parish of Aka alias Rock

---

* Deputy Recorder of Bewdley.

† Afterwards Bishop of Winchester.

‡ See *Miscellanea.*

Matrimonie or Marriages with Publications, in the Parish of Ribsford.

Such persons whose Publications are not mentioned were married by the Justices of Bewdley*

1660 Sept. 15. William Willis & Susanna Inett †

1670 Jan. 14. Mr Nathanaell Williams high Schoolemaster and Mrs Mary Boraston. Licence

1680 Aug. 26. Walter Pallmer & Ann Pooley. Licence

1688 Aug. 23. Israell Wilks & Sarah Palmer. ‡ Licence

1700 Jan. 13. Pinson Wilmot of the parish of Kidderminster & Anne Woods Spinster married by Mr Thomas Boraston curate of Bewdley at Ticknell without my leave and unknown to me till after the wedding was over

1716 Jan. 16. Wm Pountney widower aged above 70 and Margaret Moorley widow aged (as some say 84, others 89 and others 93) both of this parish. There were present as 'twas judged 500 spectators

Burials.

1660 April 7. Charles son of John Crump killed by the fall of the bodie of a dungway reared up to the wall of ye King's Stable

1661 Sept. 4. Mr Walter Pooler, Fellow of Trinity Coll. Oxon

Dec. 19 John Johnson, stabbed into the shoulder by his wife, wherof hee died, for which she was buried at Worcester

1663 Mr George Lowe High Schoolmaster

1667 Thomas More Gent born at More in Shropshire

1669 Philip son of Philip Payne

1676 March 3. A stranger found dead by a hay-rick

March 16. Anne daughter of Mrs Elizabeth Perot widdowe

1677 March 3. John Allen, a walking man

1709 James Durrham one of the serjeants of this corporation

Mary Bliss (who poisoned herself)

1713 John Coley an Anabaptist. Buried at the Quaker's Meeting House

Mr. John Amphlett an eminent Chirurgeon

1714 William Cowper drowned in Roger Paine's draw-well

1719 June 17. William Rogers Waterman [an excom. person not buried with the Burial Office]

1719 Oct. 4. Robert Herriton, Maltster [murdered]

---

* During the Commonwealth persons could be married by Justices of the Peace after the banns had been published at the Market Cross by the Town Crier.

† Parents of Bishop Willis.

‡ Grandparents of the notorious John Wilkes.

Bewdley Chapel & Bridge Wardens' Accounts.

1569	Pd to the Curat or Chapelyn in payment of his half yeres stypend due at the feast of St Michell the Archangell in the 10th yere of the sd sovereign lady the Queene	vl xs
	Pd for the half yeres rent of his house	iijs ivd
1570	Item Pd for white Incle* for the Bybull	id
	Item Pd for 2½ yds of greene cotton to cover the Seate where the Counsaill† sitteth	ivs vid
	Pd for an homyny‡ book agst the Rebels	xiid
1571	Pd to Edw. Haward for my Lord Vicnt Harf.§ a drinking	vs
	Pd in the Church to the Plaiers	xvid
	Pd to John Millard for wine wh. was given to Mr Justice Throkmorton	xviiid
	Pd for gathering oister shells to the bridge..	iid
1572	Recd of Edw. Baker for his standing under the Stepell ..	xxd
	Recd of Mr Hill and Mr Fooller for the Church Vestments	iijl vis viiid
	Pd unto Mr Drax for the Communion Cuppe	ivl ivs
	Pd to Mr Recevr for postage money..	viiis
	Pd for mending the paule	ivd
	Pd for a napkin to the Challis	
	Pd to Thos Newey for 5lb. of lead	vid
	Pd unto the Alle Wife at Ovr Areley for our dinners when we sett down the stonnes	vid
	Pd unto Wm Smythe the laborer for 10 daies work about the bridge	vs
	Pd unto Mr Sheriffe's men for the mearsement‖ of the towne	lis

* Incle, an inferior kind of tape.
† The Council of the Marches of Wales.
‡ A homily book against the Rebels in the North.
§ Viscount Hereford.
‖ Amercement.

1572	Pd unto John Hayley for bandinge the church box ..	ijs
	Pd unto Rd Bonkenell for a new bucket to the towne well	vd
	Pd for two horse load of lyme	xvid
	Pd unto the quenes plaiers in the church	vis viijd
	Pd unto Mr Heward of the Crowne at my Lord Byshoppe of Worcester's being here	iijs ivd
	Pd unto Edw. Haward for wine at my Lord of Leyster's Commissioners being here	xvid
	Pd unto Wm Griffin for Sir Thos Russell with the other Commissoners for there dinners	xis
	Pd unto John Hayley for the Bonniers drinking at the Bonfyers accg to the old custom	ivd
	Pd unto the Sheriffe for amersement about Stinkes ..	xs
1573	Pd for Wyne and Suger to make my Lorde Byshop drinke	vis viijd
	Pd to my Lorde of Lester's pleyars *	viijs
	Pd for the forfet of our Register Boke to the Queen's Commysoners at Limster	xijd
1574	Pd to Henry *Glashyer* for *glasinge* the chappell †	xxvijs
	Pd for Wyne for my Lords kynsman that preched ..	ixd
1575	For a hogsed of wyne given to Syr John Hubots ‡ ..	vl
1576	For paving at the Bolrynge §	iiid
1577	For wyne & sugar when the Justes was heare at the mouster	iis xd
	For a marked strycke	xxd
	To put the scholemaster's chambers in order	iis viiid
1578	Pd to William Lake for mending the gomestoole ‖ ..	ivd

* These players visited Stratford-on-Avon the same year.

† A good instance of word-making, and of the origin of proper names.

‡ Sir John Huband or Hibbots, of Ipsley, Warwickshire, Steward to the Earl of Leicester: one of the donors of the Mill and Meadow Money.

§ Bull Ring.

‖ Cucking stool to "duck" scolding women. The word is spelt Gronncyll, Gounstole, Gomstole (1584), Gomeble Stoole (1588), Gombell Stoole (1618). The Leominster ducking stool is still preserved, and was last used in 1817. The object of the ducking stool is thus described by Vincent Bourne:—

"Near many a stream was wont to meet us
A Stool, to broils a sure quietus.
It curb'd the tongue, the passions rein'd,
And Reason's empire firm maintained.
Astride it set up but a Xanthippe,
Then twice or thrice virago dip ye;
And not a lambkin on the lea
Will leave the stream more meek than she.
A Lethe o'er her memory shed,
The very shades of anger fled.
Cool grows the fever of the breast,
And surging passions seek to rest.
The lesson *ex cathedra* taught
Here balance in the scale of thought;
Then say if e'er Socratic school
Such lesson taught as Ducking Stool."

1578	Pd to my lorde Smythe* to help the Rowcaster† ..	vid
	Pd for six quartes of wynne when my lord landed at Syverne side	iiis
	Payed for half a pound of suger	xd
1579	Payed Wm. Lake for mending the pyllery	iiiid
	Pd for 2 daies work to whitlime the chappell	xxd
	Pd to my lorde Smyth for helping ii daies	xiid
1580	Pd for Rushes and franckynsence for my Lordes seate ..	iid
1582	for 2 quarts of Claret for my Lord Sidney‡	iis vid
1583	Recd half yeres rent for Setes in the chapel	il iiis vid
	[Seven at 2s. 6*d*. and three at 2s.]	
	Pd to Wm Smith for Key to the Workehouse	ivd
1585	Pd the Register for staying the apparence at Tenbury in byinge a Bibell	xviiid
	for fyve skins for mending of the Organ	iis vid
	for feching the crouner § and gave hym a quart of wyne ..	xiiid
1587	Pd unto Mr Drax for 15½lbs. of suger yt was given to my Lorde p'sydent ‖	xxvs
	For 20 querles¶ of new glass	iiis
1589	paide for ringinge when the Spanniardes shipes were taken in Irelande**	xvid
	Pd to the Bally for mirrimente	vid
	Paid in chardges when my yonge Lord was here ..	xvis
1592	Pd for carriage of 4000 tyle from Bristol	xivs
	Tiles for paving the chapel	xxviiil viiis
	Pd for the drinking bestowed on the Cowtis of Lecester ..	xiis ivd
1593	Pd for a new Com'nion Boke	ivs ivd
	Pd for a new dree for the bucket of the towne well ..	ivd
	Pd to Edw. Gosnell for lyme att tymes when we could gett no Clee lyme	viis
	Pd to Richard Barnsley for wardinge a week	iijs
	Pd unto the glasier for mendinge the glasse at the greate winde in the chappell	xxd
	Pd to my Lord President†† his players	xxs
	Pd for a galland of beere given to the Beishopp of Hereford	iiijd
	Pd for a pottell of wyne and suger and metheglin‡‡ given to docter lewys	iis ivd

* Deformed persons are said to have been called "my lord." (Prattinton).
† Roughcaster.
‡ Sir Henry Sidney, Lord President of the Marches.
§ Coroner.
‖ Henry Earl of Pembroke.
¶ Diamond-shaped panes.
** Wreck of the Spanish Armada.
†† Henry Earl of Pembroke.
‡‡ Drink made from honey.

1593	Pd for a new Com'nion booke	ivs ivd
	For a bottell of Clarett wine wh. Oswould Stookes gave to Mr. Acton* to gett leave to have woodd and licence to make a Cabbin in the parke for the sycke people†	xiiiid
1594	Pd to Mr Chambers of Worcester for 9½ ells of fine clothe for a Surplisse & for the making thereof	xxxs ixd
	Pd to William Millton to make upp the Booke for Stratforde	xviiid
	Pd for a sheete and other things about the buryinge of one that dyed in the king's stable‡	xvid
	Pd for making of the chamber in the Almeshouse for ould Hatton's wyfe	iiis viiid
	Pd for mendinge of a bauldricke and oyle for the clocke and for liquor for the bells	vid
	Pd to John Glover for nayles & leather to binde downe certayne mattes in the Deputyes seate and in the two Chauncells§ and for Rushes and for washinge the surplesse and table cloathe att another tyme.. ..	xiiiid
1595	Recd att St. Andrewes fayre fr. pewterers	xiis
	For smale standings	viis
	Rd at St. George his fayre	iis
	Rd at St. Annes fayre	iis vid
	Pd for digginge of xxvii loades of stone to pave in the parke lane and at tynker's gate and att the Bridge and att Severne Bridge	vis ixd
	Pd to John Draper for v ounces of fringe for the pulpitt cloath	xiis vid
	Pd for two skeynes of sylke and for vi yards of greene Inckle	vid
	Pd for settinge it and bindinge it aboute	vid
	Pd to the Ringers on the queenes hollyday & for a pound of candells	iis
	Pd for washing the table cloathe agaynst Easter	iid
1596	for a Prayer Booke from the Ld Bp of Hervarte	ivd
	for a Planke to mend the hole out of the Chancell into Mersour Tavarn‖..	xvid
	Recd of Rychard bryan the flecher¶	xxxvis viiid

* Owner of Ribbesford.

† A plague in 1593: the Ribbesford registers show 202 burials in that year: usual number about 35.

‡ The King's stable appears to have been used as a refuge for "casuals."

§ There were three *chantries* in the chapel previous to the Reformation.

‖ There were houses *under* the chancel.

¶ Arrow maker.

1596	Pd to John Glover for the Ringers at the coming in of my Lord President *	ixd
	Pd for things that were given to the Countes † by the towneswomen	xl is
	Pd for Mr Justes Shuttleworthes dyet & horsmeate ..	xxvs viiid
1597	Pd the 3rd of Aprill Mr Sweeper's wages the first payment	£1
	Pd to the constable Thomas Hill that was geven for the rausomyng of soulders	iiis ivd
	A Suger Lofe given to Sir John Pakenton the 30 of July 1597 waying x lbs iii oz at xxd the lb	xviis
	Pd to Thomas Haiward the 4 November for the dyett and horsemeat for the Steward Mr Morgan and others of my Lords gentlemen	xliis xd
	for xi fotte of bords to mend on the top of the stepell ..	iiis ivd
	Pd at the coming in of my Lord to the Towne & for ringing the first of May	xviiid
1598	Pd for things geven to the Countes the 6 of June 1598 by the towneswomen i suger lofe xvs vid iiii boxes of marmalat ixs viiid ii boxes of comfets vs: som ..	xxxs iid
	Receyved in pt that the women pay'd towards their som iis vid a pece being vii women amounting to xviis vid rest to paye	
	Pd John Glover for filling the holes at tycknill that the plomer left undone	iiid
	For iiij yards of grene . . . to laye one the desk that the Justes leans one in the Court House	iiis viiid
	Pd the 28th October 1598 to a precher	iiis
	Pd to Mr Millward that was geven to Mr Roper's man for writing letter	iis
	Pd to Henry Smyth for carreg of the same letter to Willton ‡	xiis ivd
1599	Pd to Mr Southall & Mr Knype the 5 of September 1599 to goe to Lichfield about the survaur of the schole house	xxs
	Pd for paynts (?) geven to the scolers	viiid
	For corten rings tenter hokes to hang the clothes in the Court House	iid
1600	Pd to John Wilkes the 12 of May 1600 by Mr Cowpur appoyntment for the hier of a horse to Lichfield about the survaur of the schole house..	

* Henry Earl of Pembroke.

† Countess of Pembroke.

‡ The Earl of Pembroke's seat in Wiltshire.

1600 Recd for ii standyngs betwixt the Condet & the Well .. iis ivd

Recd of a sault woman at the poule.. .. .. .. xvid

To my ptner Clare the first of March 1600 when Mr Coulson went to Ludlow about the schole lands Mr Hill gave .. .. xvs

Pd to Mr John Mylward in pte of his dett the 7 of November 1600 the chardges of Justes Luttner at his house .. .. xxxvs iiid

Pd the same tyme for Ringing for the Erle of Pembroke . iis

Pd to John Monox for mending to stope out the boyes in the lofte in the church, and nayles .. .. .. iiid

Pd the 12 of March 1600 for cloth to shroud a pore child dyed in the king's stabell xid. in money for the women to bury him .. .. vid

Pd 26 March 1601 for a payer of hooks and hinges for one of the wast doors of the Condet in the parke.. .. xd

1601 Pd for plankes and bords & noggs* for the walls iii

Pd to Mr Yardley for his quarter's wages .. .. .. xls

Pd to Dolittle of Kethermoster for the quenes rent .. iiijs

Pd for the charges bestowed on Mr Justes as he came throu the town .. .. xs iid

Pd for a days worke for on man at Higley for playnynge ston .. .. xvid

Pd for skowringe the sestorn at ticknell and mending the pipes.. .. .. iijd

Pd for makinge the horse bridge in Dog lane and carege of the timber & for the timber .. .. xiiiis viiid

Recd the Stipente money the fees beinge allowde owt of the same .. .. viil vis viiid

Recd of the widdow Bell for the Bridge House .. .. xs

Recd of Eleanor . . . for the Lower Rowme of the Bridge House .. .. iis vid

1602 Recd of the Saltwoman for her standinge at the somer poule for the half year .. .. viiid

The same year there was on Joane Moare gave for her cominge into the Almshous .. .. xs

the which was bestowed on the Reparynge of the sayd Almshouse by Richard Clare

For Reparinge the Condet in the parke and in Harry Woods garden and in Ticknell .. .. ijs ijd

Pd to Wm. Smallman for two quartes of Claret wine and suger at the cominge of Sir Thomas Layton.. .. xxd

Pd for wine & suger & cakes at the comynge of my Lord†

---

* Noggs—filling up of the interstices of a building composed partly of wood.—*Halliwell.*

† Lord Zouch.

1602	to Ticknell	xviis iid
	Pd to John Monox and his man for makinge the Brige at Bark hill..	iis xd
	Pd to Thomas Mylls for sawinge the timber & making the sawpit & filling up the sawpit	iijs xd
	Pd unto Greenbanke of Worcester for mendinge the nether Condet & the over Condet	xxxivs xd
	Pd for diggınge of ston in Hitrell and layinge the same & mendinge of a mattocke	iis
	Pd for ringinge at the Lord cominge	iis
	for strawinge the Churche	vjd
1603	Pd for a hondred of brike to amend on of the chimnes upon the bridge & for stones & gravel to pave on the bridge & for workmanshipe	vis vjd
	Pd toe the Clarke of the market for his good will.. ..	xs
	For Ringinge on Sainte James daye and for Ringinge on the kinges hollyday For ringinge for my Lordes coming to towne Item for mendinge the Balldrigges of the bells	iiijs iid
	For mendinge the benche in the Chancell	id
	Pd to Dowles of Bromsgrove for vii Kaggesmentes* ..	xviis vid
	Pd for Bayes, tacks & Incle for my L. his sett	iiis iiid
	Pd for the paynting of the Chauncell	xxd
	Pd to Richard Clare for the repereing of Stenfort Bridge †	xxxs
	Pd for the amending of the Cook in the Bruhouse in Tycknelle	xviid
	Pd for the takyng awaye of William Woosloyes child owtt of this towne—and he did enter in to band that the towne sholld not be trobled noe more withe hit ..	xs
	Pd owte of the Stipendary money to Alderman Kinges offecers	xviis vid
	Pd for mendinge of the coke of the greate condeth in the towne	iis vjd
1604	Pd to them that playd on the waytes at the cominge in of the Lord Zowche	iis
	Pd to the Ringers at the same time	xiid
	Pd for on statewte booke conserning the poore people ..	iis vid
	the charges to answer the Justesses conserninge upton brige	iis xd
	Payde for a newe booke of Com'on prayer Set owte by Acte of parlemente of the greate Vollon ‡	viis viiid

* Casements (?).

† Humphrey Pakington, of Over Sapey, built Stanford Bridge in 1548, and it is still repaired by Dodingtre Hundred.

‡ Hampton Court Conference this year.

1605	Pd for a new booke of Iniuncions	xvid
	for a stock to sett the kinges boord on	viid
	for on sewger lofe to geve the Lorde Zowche	xxs
	for the charges bestowed on Sir Richard Lewkner & his company	iiil xs iid
	for a flagon pot of tine for the Church	vis ivd
	Pd to Mr Morres for his wages beinge three quarters ..	vil
	Pd for payntinge the Chapell..	xlixs
	For shingle to the Scoole howse beinge two thousand wantinge halfe a hondered	xlvs
	For the kepinge of a child to the widow nickols	il iiis vid
	For shingle more to the Scool howse of the newe buildinge being 2000	xlvs
	Bestowed on the Lord Bishop at his going to Ludlow ..	iiis ivd
	Bestowed on Mr hussey the kinges Commissioner ..	ijs
	Item for on hoggshed of beer..	xviis
1606	Pd to Thomas Webe for a timber pece to make the whiping stokes	viiid
	Pd to Mr Milward to goe to Sur Edward Bluntes to Kitherminster	iiis ivd
	Pd to Omfry Hamons for lending a payer of boutes ..	iiijd
1607	for mending the cunstables stafe	vd
	for mendinge the brige at wimbrucke	vid
	for the beare at my Lordes cum'ing	xiiiis vid
	Pd for the kinges holiday last beinge the v November 1607*	iiis vid
	Pd for wine when the Judges whent throw the towne ..	ivs ivd
	Recd of Jeffri Pardo for pichin pence for the faier ..	xxivs
	The charge of Sir Edward Blunt's suit concerning the court leete & Towne howse amounteth to £10 4*s*. 8*d*. as appeareth by a pticular	
	To Mr Haward for the leather seale	viijs
	for rushes & flowers	vd
	for fringe for my Lords seate..	vid
	Mr Whitcot hath laide out to the muster-master for keepinge of the sicke people, & for wardinge wh. is to be levied by the Towne	37s 8d
1611	to John Glover for rossin, tallow, pipe, lead and salte with other necessary things	xxd
	for mending the stayer dore in the Chappell	ijd
	To Hugh Lowe for money wch he layd out for mendinge of the prison house at the bridge	vs
	To Thomas the cutler for scouring of holbeards at St Andrewes tide	xxd
	To Hugh Clare on christmas day for mending one of the mases	xviiid

* Gunpowder plot 1605.

1611	for a debenter for the townes buisnes for the Curat of the Chappell of Bewdley	iiis ivd
	for the change of the Curat's name	xiid
	To Hugh Lowe for riding to London on the townes buisness	xxs
	To Wm Glover for his horse	xis
	Pd to Mr Moris & Mr Underhill for one whole yeare	viiil
	Pd to Will. Keye for the use of xxl wch was due at April last 1611 *	iil
	To Boult for drawinge Interogatories agynst the Bishops at Easter tearme	vs
	To a boye for clearinge claye out of dog lane	iid
	To John Glover for mendinge the Conduit the viiith of ffebruary beinge broken in four places after the great frost 1610	xvis
	For three fathom of belrope	vid
	To John Glover for ringing the schollers bell this two yeares ended at St Mary day last 1612 †	xxs
	Payd to Hugh Lowe for wine & cakes at my Lord riding through the Towne	iiis ivd
	To Mr Brasier the same tyme for beare	iiis ivd
	To Mr Chelmicke for enroulinge the Cope [copy] of the surveie ‡	vs
	Recd of Richard Gardner for a fraye & bloudshed wch he made xs whereof Mr Brasier had iis	viiis
	Pd to Mr Simons for a coppy of the enditement wch. Heyward pfered agaynst us for the market bushell and for takinge toule on the bridge	xiis
	Pd for the charges of the Com'ssion betwixt Sir Edward Blunt & the Towne for the Commissioners dinners & the witnesses	vs iiiid
	Pd for dinner for vi persons	iiis
	Pd the same tyme for wine	iiid
	Pd to Mr Bayliffe to send up to Mr Bromley at Hillari Tearme for suites in law betwixt Sir Edward Blount & the Towne	xls
1613	for haye to laye under the gutter	jd
	To Mr Doctor Gryffithes for fees to answere the excommunication for Mr Tombes & John Hardwicke	is xd

* Interest 10 per cent.

† This bell was rung at five o'clock in the morning to call the scholars of the Grammar School to their studies. It was continued till 1801, when it was considered a nuisance, and called forth the following epigram by W. P.:

> "Ye rascally ringers, ye merciless foes,
> Who persecute every friend to repose:
> I wish for the quiet and peace of the land,
> You had round your necks what you hold in your hand."

‡ Prince Henry's Survey. See Chapter 1.

1613	for a payre of skales and a leaden waight to waie butter	is xd
	For the certiffying in the writte for the burgisse of the parlamt and the carriage	20s
	To Mr Draper for cloth to make the bellmans cote ..	viiis
1614	For two shrowdes for two poore folke at the apointment of Mr Bayliff Smith	iis
	For two postes & two plankes to make the stockes ..	iiiis vid
	To fyve wardens at St Andrewes fayer	vis
	To Willm Newie for skouring harnis	is vid
	To the turner of the wyer hill for turning 3 dozen of pyllers	iiis iiid
	To Mr Chelmicke at his going to London for to sue for the towle of the markett by the consent of the Bayleiff and Burgesses	iiil xs
	To Rich. Wowen for a horse to carrie Sowthall to bromigium* for a witnesse about the towle of the markett	iis
	To Mr Prince for an atturneys fee	iis
	To Mr Heath for his quarters wages at midsomber 1615.	iil
	In expenses at Ludlow when I rode thyther to follow the sute betwixt the towne & Cooke, mie selfe† & mie horse three dayes	vs
	For the turninge of the pillers of the Church‡	iiis
1615	To Hugh Low for wine that was bestowed upon mie Lord psedent at his last being in Bewdley	xis viiid
	To Mr Cliffe when he sate on the Commission betwixt the Towne & Sir Fran. Lacon	xis o
	To Mr Ralph Smith for diet & horsmeate for the Commissioners & the witnesses	iiil o o
	for the skouring of eight houlbeards and one . . . byll against the assizes 1616	iis o
	Rd Dallow for wine bestowed on Sir Francis Evers ..	iiis ivd
	Given to mie lordes chamberline Mr Baylis when the lease was scaled betwene Sr Edward Blount & the towne	oo vs
	To the yeoman of the wardrobe	oo is
	Given to mie lordes players	oo xs
	Pd for the carriage of one loade of the councells stuffe ..	jl iiis iid
	Pd for a Chamber for Mr ffowler when the sises§ were held in Bewdley	oo xs oo
	Pd to Mr Corbitt the muster-master	oo xs oo
	Given to Thomas Dovie & to Thomas Boylsonne to presse them for traine souldiers..	oo iis

* Old pronunciation of Birmingham. Cf. Dowles Registers, 1674.

† Robert Vicaris.

‡ A new gallery in the chapel. § Assizes.

1615	Pd to Stephen Grove wch. he recovered by an order from the Councell against the toune	viiil
1616	Imprimis pd to Richard Dallowe for Entertaininge the Cheife Justice Three severall times	xxiiis
	For entertayninge Sir ffrauncis Eure cheife recorder ..	xxxxs
	Pd to Mr Wright for one quarter's service	xxxxs
	Pd to Mr Wright for the hire of twentie pounds wch was given to the free schoole..	xs
1617	Pd at Mr Baylif's comand to the Kings Trumpeters ..	xis
	Pd for the timber & iron worke for the pillory and gombell stowle	il iiis vid
	for makinge the pillory & gombell stowle	xvs xd
	Pd Mr Smith for my Lordes diette & horse meat	xil iiis ivd
	For a pottell of bornt sacke to make the Justis drinke ..	iis viiid
	to make the whipinge poste	is viiid
	for mending the plompe in the over street *	xid
1620	Recd of John Soley for a seate for his wife being the third seate on the north side of the chappell	00 02 06
	Pd for the sweeping of the streetes	00 01 00
	for a linke & staples for the bridghouse	00 00 09
	to Goodman Mansfeild for business he did for the towne	00 00 04
	for timber hinges and a board for the Court house at the Stags head	00 02 07
	For nine yards and a haulfe of wainescott, to Wm Paine for seates in the Church, & for setting oup of dores in the woomens seates & for boards to make seates and for three matts and nailes	01 02 00

A note of money recd & disbursed by us Will. Hopkins and John Soley by appoint. & consent of the bayleif and Burgisses as followeth

Imp.	Recd of Mr John Hamonds pson of Ribbesfourd wch was lefte by Mr Barber Mr of the late Lotterie in Bewdley to be imployed to such charitable uses in the said Towne as should be thought fitt by the said bayleife and burgisses at the oversight of the said Mr Hamonds the sum of	xxivl 00s 00d
It.	Rec. of John Clare late Bridgwarden as by his accompts will appear the sum of	vil 00 00

A note how the said monney was disbursed.

Imps Paid to Mr Edmond Boylsonne by the appointment of the said Bayleife & burgisses the daie and yeare abovesaid to discharge Mr Edward Tombes from an

* Now called High Street.

order wch. the said Mr Boylsonne had against him for money that the Towne had received .. .. xxl 00 00

It. paid to the said Mr Tombes to redeeme the Toule of the marketts & fayers out of his hands by the consent of the said bayleif and burgisses the sum of .. .. xxl 00 00

ffor the wch. said xxiiijl it was agreed by the said Companie that the sum of fowertie shillings p annum should for ever * be paide to the schoolemaster of the free gramer schoole of the said Towne and unto the poore of the same viz. :—twentie shillings p ann. to either of them at the feast of the nativitie of St John baptist and the nativitie of our Lord God by eaven & equall portions; & that out of the Towle of the said markett & faire. Whereupon the said money was disbursed as aforesaid

James Nash gent—Bayliff	Mr Will. Hopkins
Richard Whitcott gent	Mr Silvanus Sares
William Milton gt	Mr Edmond Boylsonne
William Hayles gent	John Clare gent
	Will. Harris
	Walter Pooller
	John Hales

Vicesimo septimo die Decembris: Jacobi decimo nono. 1621.

It. the daie & yeare abovsaid the said Bayleife and burgisses did consente & agree, that whereas there was the sum of twentie pounds given by one Hugh Pooller gent deceased to be imployed to the use and towards the mainetenance of the said free gram'er schoole wch said sum of xxl was in like sorte laid out in the behaulf of the said Towne; that the sum of fowertie shillings should in like manner be paide to the schoolemaster of the saide schoole yearly for ever; & that out of the pfitts of the said Towle of the marketts & fayers, at the said feast of St John the baptist & the nativity by eaven & equall portions as aforsd. †

Received for womens seates in the chappell 1619 Mr John Tiler beinge Bayliffe Mr Edward Tombes & John Clare beinge bridgewardens

[24 names at prices varying from 3*s*. 4*d*. to 2*s*.]

William Spilsbury.. .. .. iis iid
ffrancis Gilding ‡ .. .. .. iis vid
John Wowen .. .. .. iis vid
John Soley .. .. iis vid

* The payment was discontinued in 1749 without any reason given.

† This payment was also discontinued in 1749.

‡ One of the donors of the Mill and Meadow Money.

1622	Recd of John Nashe the glover for his rent	00	10	00
	,, Richard Cooke glover ,, ...	00	03	04
	of John Grove for his haulfe yeares rent for his house and for the hornas chamber	00	04	00
	Recd of the woman that selleth salte at the sumer poule	00	00	08
	Recd of Goodman Cooke for the barbours shop	00	10	00
1623	Mr Hopkins recd of Barnaby Davis to be free to sett up his trade of a chandler	01	01	04
	Pd for a pottell of Burnte sacke wch the Companie bestowed upon the Lord Psedent at his coming through Beawdley the 15th of November 1621 ..	00	02	08
	for a flagon of Beare wch the Companie dranke at the George staying for the Wine	00	00	02
	Pd to Mr Madstard for his wages	00	15	00
	For the fee due to our Cheif Recorder Sir James Whittlocke wch we paid him upon the 14th of January 1621	01	02	00
	for a suger loffe at the same time wch by the consent of the Company we did bestowe upon mie Ladie Whittlocke	00	12	06
	Pd to Thomas Pallmer of Hyggley for fiveteene tonns of stonne and for the drawinge of them to the water syde	01	10	00
	Pd to Jefferis for helping to roule stones out of Seaverne	00	00	02
	Pd for lynks & shakols for the use of the Bayleif for time being	00	02	06

It was agreed with John Little the 7th of Julie 1622 to take down the piles that were not taken downe, & to repaier the Bridge from end to end so farr as the freeston work goeth: and to maintaine & keepe the same for three yeares next ensuinge the date heareof, and at the end of the said tearme to leave it sufficientlie repayred in every respect for all wch he finding all manner of stuffe he is to have £26 wherof £05 must remaine till the third yeare.

1623	Pd to Captaine Dallowe for wine and oringes bestowed upon the Lord Psedent* at severall times	00	19	04
	For Irons to seale bushels & other measures	00	02	06
	Pd to Thomas Paine for setting a raile upon mie Ladies seate.. :	00	00	03
	It. Pd by appointment of the bayleife and burgesses for the charges when the venison was eaten at Captaine Dallows, the wch Sir James Whitelocke bestowed upon the towne	03	06	08
	It. More pd to Captaine Dallow for one hoggshed of claret wine the wch was bestowed upon the Lord p'sident	05	12	06

* The Earl of Northampton.

1623	It. paid by the appointmt of the bayleif and burgesses for pouder and matches for the souldiers when the Lord Comton* came out of Spaine	00	07	04
	It. Pd to Mrs Dallow the 11th of October for wood to make a bonfier	00	01	00
	For pouder & matches the same daie	00	08	00
	It. distributed to the poore when the mill monney was dealt in december 1622: out of the pfitts of the money that Mr Seabright & Mr Barber gave.. ..	01	00	00
1624	Recd of Thomas Richards mercer for his Coppie of freedom	03	06	08
	of Edward Wheeler for the haulf yeares rent of the little house under the stayers	00	02	00
	Pd for a planke to mend ovr the dungion where the prisoners broke out	00	00	10
	It. pd for one Ale quarte and one wine pinte sysed and sealed by the standart accordinge to the Statute the 18th of December to sise the measures withall ..	00	02	10
	Pd to Mr Owen of Ketherminster for makinge a memoriall of the bread & money that Mr Seabright† gave to the poore of this towne; to be kept in the Chappell.	00	06	08
	It. more paid to Mr Blunt for the Imblasoninge of the arms of Mr Seabright	00	02	04
	For a pottell of Clarett wine bestowed upon Mr Steward of the Councell	00	01	04
	Pd to John Clark glasier for a glasse to sett out Mr Seabright his memoriall	00	00	10
	Pd for a new statute book of the Largest Volume to remaine to the bayleif for the time beinge for ever ..	01	15	09
	Pd to Mr Ralph Clare‡ his servt for his paynes in bringing the Bucke wch. he bestowed upon the Bayleif & Burgesses 1624	00	05	00
	Pd to Samuell Oakes for making five pasties thereof, & for other meat pvided when it was eaten & for wine.	03	13	04
	Pd to make the Cheif Justis drink in wine..	00	02	08
	Pd for a quart of sack and a quart of Clarett to make mie Lord drinke at the Bridge	00	01	08

* Lord Compton, eldest son of the Earl of Northampton.

† Sir William Seabright, founder of Wolverley School: Cf. Ribbesford Registers, 1615.

‡ Sir Ralph Clare, of Kidderminster, Lessee of the Manor of Bewdley, and Member 1623—1640.

		£	s	d
1624	Recd for the Toule of the markett for two yeares.. ..	20	00	00
	of Will Woofe of Ombersley for his rent due for on house & close situate upon the Wier hill over against John Johnson's, sometimes called the little almshouse	00	15	00
	Pd to Samuel Oakes for Sir Thomas Chamberline his servts charges and horsmeat when he came down to goe to the Councell upon the removall of Sir James Whitelocke..	02	12	02
	It. Laid out in the dressinge of the venison that mie Lord p'sedent bestowed upon the town September 1624			
	to the pties that brought it down	00	02	00
	for five leggs of mutton	00	04	02
	for five neats tongues	00	02	10
	for a brisket of beife	00	02	10
	for apples peares and nutts	00	00	08
	for six pecks of wheaten flower	00	06	00
	for on pound of pepper	00	02	02
	for fower quarts of Butter	00	05	04
	For three dossen of bread	00	03	00
	For two couple of rabbits	00	01	00
	for two couple of Chickens	00	01	02
	for beare..	00	10	02
	for spices carrotts & salt	00	00	10
	for wine the same time	00	17	00
	for a pottell of Clarett & suger bestowed on mie Lords gent that came downe after dinner	00	02	00
	for a hoggshed of Clarett wine bestowed upon mie Lord psedent at the ffeast of the nativity 1624	06	03	04
	Pd to mie brother Boylson when he went to London to paie Sir James Whitelocke his fee & to answer the said sute	04	00	00
	Pd to Wm Paine for wainescott and dores to the seates next unto the little Chancell on the north side of the Chappell	01	12	00
	It. We agreed with the goodwife browning to make cleane round about the Courthouse and to carrie awaie the muck every saterday night at ijs by the yeare wh. she is to have paid hir by vid the qr. whereof we paid hir vid beforehand and she begann hir time a week after maie day..	00	00	06
	Pd to Mr Samuell Baker for the dressinge of a Bucke that Mr Ralph Clare sent 1625	02	07	00

Year	Item	£	s	d
1625	Pd to Mr Lowe the usher of the Schole	01	10	00
	Pd to Mr Sharard & Mr Lowe the Scholemarsters	01	10	00
	Pd for making a paire of Butts* for my lord	00	05	8
	Pd 2nd of Aprill at the pclayming of the King by Mr Bayliffs appointmt for 2 dromes and a fiffe	00	02	6
1626	Pd to John Clark for keeping the Conduits to bring the water from Ticknell & to mend the leads & keep them for a whole yeare	00	12	0
	Pd to Mr Edw. Littleton Recorder his fee	01	02	0
	Pd at the appointmt of the Company when the Lo. President came about the Ryall subsidye for sack & clarett	00	03	8
	Pd for bolts & links at the appoint. of Mr Bayliffe Soley for the Bridgehouse	00	02	04
	Pd for a quart of wine & suger for Mr. William Littleton when Kitherminster men came over with their Charter	00	01	0
	Pd to John Gough for 3 dayes work for setting up of the Clock and to make a scaffold to put up the dyall	00	03	8
	Pd for mending at the Bridgehouse when the prisoners came from Ludlow	00	07	2
	Pd for a pottell of white wine & another of claret for the intertaynment of the lord president & the Lo. Compton by the Companies appointmt	00	03	4
	Pd for a Coate for the Beadle	00	05	0
	Pd to the Bellfounder for the casting of the Bell	07	04	0
	For a lock to put upon the Schole house dore in the Chappell	00	00	6
	Pd for the Copie of Mr Sares will†	00	09	0
1630	to John Monnox Laborer for 23 daies worke about the recastinge of the Chappell [About £18 spent]	00	15	04
	Pd for the newe Bible for the Chappell and caridge of him from London	02	15	0
	Pd to Thomas Nashe for a large cagement to be set in the window over the Lorde Presidents pue	00	05	0
	For paintinge of the Chappell and washing of the plaisteringe	02	13	4
	Pd to Mr Thos Chamberlaine Undersheriffe to forbeare to levy £25 upon the Towne in his charge	02	00	0

* The old archery-ground is still called the "Butt-town" meadow.

† In 1826 the Churchwardens of Bewdley contributed £10 towards the repair of his monument in Nettlestead church, Suffolk. The inscription on it runs:—"In memorie of Samuel Sayer Esq. sometime of London, who built a faire almeshouse at Bewdley in Wostershire, for six poore men, and gave thirty pounds a yeare for ever to maintaine them; He departed the first of September Anno Dom. 1625."

1630	Receipts for Seates in the chappell			
	Of John Wilkes mercer	00	03	00
	of John Willis..	00	02	06
	Of Robert Pardoe	00	02	06
	&c. &c.			
	Pd for two gallons of wine bestowed upon Serient Liegh when we moved him aboute gettinge of our ordinances to be confirmed by the Lo. Keeper	00	04	00
	Pd Mr ffrauncis Walker for the exemplificacion of the Verdict against Jo: Barker Viccar of Cleobury ..	00	12	00
	Pd to Mr John Hailes for his travile and charges in ridinge to London about the *quo warranto*	03	00	00
	More due to me* when I had the Royaltie of the mannor for v yeares and a halfe from the Towne, for Rent for the Towne Land at xis per ann.	02	17	06
1631	Pd for ale for them wch removed the butter crosse ..	00	02	04
	Pd to Mr Milton for timber to make a dorment in the butter crosse	00	04	00
	Pd for haire for the Chappell..	00	01	06
	Pd for mendinge of the Bridge	06	10	00
	Pd to John of Barkhill for one yeares wages for sweepinge the streets	00	08	00
	Pd for a shovle to make them cleane	00	01	00
	Pd for beere bestowed upon the Ringers at the birth of Prince Charles	00	00	06
	Pd for passinge of a Surrendor for the land whereon the hospitall stands	00	02	00
1632	Pd to Mr Blayne the preacher	06	00	00
	Pd for a Curbe for the buckett for the well on the sandy banke	00	17	10
	Pd for a sir loyne of beef and a briskett, a quarter of lambe, a quarter of veale and a quarter of mutton by Mr Bayliffs and his bretherens appointment to psent Sir Henrye Herbert	00	15	00
	Pd for two gallons of wine when the Townsmen went to Sir Hen: herbert to Ribbesford	00	04	00
	Pd Edward Walker for an houre glasse for the Chappell.	00	00	08
	Pd for 3 pottles of wine, whereof one was sack, and half a pound of suger, wch was bestowed upon the Lo: Willoughby as he came through the Towne	00	04	10
	Pd for a booke to be used upon the gunpowder Treason daye	00	00	8

* Edward Boylsonne.

1632	Pd Mr Sharard for the new butter crosse, being Mr Whittcoats gift	00	08	03
	Pd to Oldberry in earnest of the bargaine to cast the bell.	00	01	00
1633	Pd for taking downe of the great bell, for drawing him to the water & carriadge up & downe and for the over-plus mettell..	13	02	03
	Pd Mr Milton for a plank to mend the bridge at Tuckers gate & for shingles & lathes	00	09	02
	[The pew rents for this year amounted to £14 11*s.* 2*d.*]			
	Pd to Mr Sharrard Curate of the Chappell for these 2 yeares	16	0	0
	Pd to Mr Sharrard being High Scholemaister	00	16	0
1634	In the Chappell for inlardging the galerye making the new dorment the staires the pulpit & reading place and the seats through the Chappell			
	Imp. for 4 hun & 3 quarters of square Timber at xviiis viiid per hun	04	09	6
	for 600 fote of inch boards at 9*s.* 6*d.* the hundred.. ..	02	17	0
	for 291 foote of half inch boards at 11*s.* viii*d.* the hundred	01	02	4
	for 8 yards of duble rayle and a plank for inlardging of the pulpit and reading place	0	04	0
	for red lead & . . . . to colour the pulpit	0	03	7
	Pd the chardges of Mr Grayle & Mr Holland for them-selves & their horses at the George when Mr Grayle came from Gloucestr & was elected Chief Schole maister	00	10	00
	Given to Mr Needham when he came to preach for a tryall for the Curats place of the Chappell	00	06	8
	Itm Pd Mr Edwards chardges for his horsemeat when he came to preach for a tryall for the Curat's place of the Chappell	00	05	4
	Itm Pd Mr Moreton's chardges for his horsemeat & his ffrends at the Swan when he came to preach for a tryall and was elected by the bayliffe & Burgesses to be Curate for the Chappell	00	07	4
1636	Recd of Thomas Gower for his freedome	02	6	8
	For wine sent to Sir Walter Denny when the soldiers were trayned	0	3	4
	Pd to Mr Nash towards his chardges with others that went with him to Worcester at the quarter sessions about the Ship money	0	3	4

1636	Itm there is to be receaved from Mr Grayle all the entrances for forraine Schollers that he receaved into the Schole from Jan. 1, 1635, to June 24, 1637.			
	Pd to Wm Paine for cutting the Towne armes	0	4	0
	For beere for the workmen & others that holp them ..	0	2	0

Those whose names are subscribed weare at the charge of makinge the new lofte in the Chappell 1642. And were appointed to sitt there by ffrancis Bromwich and William Unckles then Chappell wardens

Nicholas ffalkner	Jonn Broadhurst	Jon Hill butcher	John Dawbery
Tho: ffalkner	Thomas Wootton	John Budd	Roger Wainwright
William Hill	Robert Barrett	John Lewis	Roger Elfes
Thomas Dovie	Jon. Glasserd	William Collins	Jon Hill the seriant's sonne

1637	Pd in going to the high Shiriffe concerning the Towne about Ship money	0	16	2
	Laid out at the Assizes attending upon the high Shiriffe about ship money	0	11	0
	Pd for wrighting the peticion..	0	01	0
	Pd Mr Hungerford wch was disbursed by him at London about Ship money..	01	15	0
	Pd for a sugar loaf for Sir Hen: Harbert	0	19	5
	Pd the undersheriffe for his paynes	01	0	0
	For wine for the lo: Bishop at the Angel	0	3	0
	for beare at the same time	0	0	2
	Pd Sr Hen: Harbt wch he disbursed at london for the Towne	7	3	8
	Pd Thos. Wood for going for schole rent to wales ..	0	4	6
	Pd for tile to use at the King's board & carriadge up the water	2	4	9
	Laid out at Whitborne about the Schole	0	3	4
1638	Money disbursed in repairing at the Conduit	3	12	1
	Pd to Wm Shawe for soder and lead & worke over the South Chauncell	0	2	6
1639	Received of 13 butchers for standings in the walk on the South side	2	15	10
	Received of 19 butchers for standings in the walk on the North side	2	12	7
	Received for rent of 16 houses and shops	8	6	10
	" for seats in the Chappell (13 names)	3	0	0
	Total for the half year	16	15	3

1639	Pd Edw. Osland towards cleansing the Towne well ..	0	0	3
	Pd Jo: Gough for fitting the poules to waye Coles ..	0	0	8
	Received at St Andurewes faire 1638 of the Brasiers & standings in the walk & butter Crosse..	3	6	3
	Pd to Tho. Stephens for chaines for the comon ballance .	0	6	0
	Pd for a bushel of peeble stones used at the bridge ..	0	2	8
	Pd Wm Bennet for sweeping the streets another quarter..	0	1	8
1639-41	Pd Jo. Lane for the Sergeants seate	0	17	0
	Pd Sam: Gosnell for mending a holbard	0	0	10
	For mending the weomens seates in the Chappell ..	0	4	8
	Pd for a carpet for the Court house table	1	2	0
	Pd for removing the gunpowder out of the Chappell into the Court house	0	0	4
	Pd Nick: Falkner for making a paire of stayers & 2 new seates in the loft	2	10	0
	Pd the Cleark at lady-day half years wages	0	10	0
	Pd Peter Rea to boat up & downe to see the defects at the Bridge	0	0	4
	Pd for a pottle of sack & a pottle of claret sent to Sr Hen: Herbert	0	3	4
	Pd Mr Blount for wrighting two copies of a Record concerning the Chappell—the one to goe to the plint & the other to remayne among the towne wrightings ..	0	4	0
	Pd for 2 bushell of Clee Lime	0	1	0
	Pd Geo. Monnox for wine bestowed on Ministers at several times	0	6	0
1642	Pd for Candells when ye soldiers did watch	0	0	6
	Pd for a drum by Mr Bayliff's appointment	0	11	6
	Pd for wine & suger for Sr Tho: Littleton	0	3	8
	Pd Mr Sares by the companyes appointmt..	4	0	0
	Pd Mr Vernons man ye fee farme rent	1	0	0
1643	Pd to Wm Hill for ye soldiers	0	2	0
	Pd for scouring 3 holbarts	0	0	9
	Pd for a paire of hartshornes & setting on..	0	0	3
	Pd Walter Tay for hanging the gattes	0	1	2
	Pd beere at ye setting of ye gates	0	0	6
	Pd for mending ye gunpowder barrell	0	0	3
	Pd for 12 lb & halfe of powder	0	16	8
	Pd for a hing to the bridge house gate	0	0	6
	Pd for a chaine for the bridge house dore	0	0	9

1643	Pd Mr Kenrick	2	10	0
	[Chapel warden: Mr John Wilkes]			
	for a hoggeshead of Claret wine for Prince Rupert ..	4	10	0
	for a pottle of sack & pottle of Claret for the lord herbert	0	3	4
	for a quart of sack & quart of Claret for Coll. Sandes *..	0	2	8
	for a pottle of sack for Sr Wm Russell	0	2	0
	for a pottle of sack for Sr Gilbt. Gerard	0	2	0
	for a pottle of sack for Maior Savage	0	2	0
	for going to Shrewsburye	4	6	0
	for wine for Coll. Washington	0	2	4
	for wine for Mr Towneshend..	0	7	4
	for squaring & cutting the Somer pole	0	1	10
1643-1645	Recd of straingers for standings in the walke for their cheese	1	6	0
	Recd at St Andrewes faier for standings of cheese at the Crosse	2	3	10
	Pd J. Vaughan for sweeping the pke lane	0	0	3
	Pd Geo. Monnox for 2 pottles of sacke and a pint sent to Sr Tho: Littleton	0	6	0
	Pd for ringing at Prince Rupert's coming	0	1	6
	Pd for ringing at the kings coming to Towne & going forth	0	2	0
	Pd for pulling downe the Bayliffs seate and setting up againe when the king was here..	0	0	6
	Pd Edw. Teigh for beere when the schole way was set out	0	0	4
	Pd Dorothy lee for beere for Mr Grayle	0	0	4
	Pd Ringers for Prince Rupert	0	1	0
	Pd for paving wch the reformadoes broke up	0	6	10
	Pd Mr Gilding 2 suger loaves..	2	4	4
1646-7	Pd for an houre glasse pro Capella	00	00	09
	Pd for another debentr for rec. of viiil	00	12	08
	Pd for matts for the Bayliffs seate	00	03	00
	Pd Mr Recordr littleton his fee for 2 years..	02	04	00
	Pd our chardges riding to Judge Wilde † to Worcsr ..	00	01	05
	Pd for beere to the Jurye that set out the schole land at the Boars head	00	01	06
	Pd Mr Borraston for an ordr about Brecknock	00	02	06

* Governor of Worcester for Charles I.

† Chief Baron of the Exchequer: drew up the impeachment against the Bishops in 1641.

1646-7	Pd Vickris for arresting of Paine	00	00	06
	Pd for sack bestowed on Maior Saunders	00	01	06
	Pd Mr Hopkins his chardges in going to London to get allowance for our Minister	02	00	00
	Pd for wine to Mr Turton to get off our men from going to worke at the Castle*	00	01	00
	Pd to Bennet for making cleane the Courthouse in the time of warr	00	01	00
	Pd for a quart of sack for Mr Davies brother the Minister	00	01	02
	Pd for wine bestowed upon Judge Wilde	00	02	08
	Pd to Jo. Hinton for tile & quarries for the Chappell ..	05	19	06
	More laid out at worcester the 21 of decem 1648 to attend the Comrs when the Countrey mett to oppose the order for chardging them	0	9	1
	Pd for wine to make the townsmen drink wth Mr Needham who did teach at the Chappell Oct. 25, 1648 ..	0	4	3
	Pd the ringers on a thanksgiving day	0	2	0
1649-1651	Pd for ringing the 5 9ber & for Ireland	0	4	0
	Pd Jo. Weaver for mending the seats & other worke done in the Chappell at the dispute	0	5	0
	Pd for cake cheese & beere at the delivering up of the former Bridgewardens accompts	0	1	7
	Pd for drawing a peticon for augmentation	0	2	6
	Pd for a quart of sack for Mr Tombes	0	1	4
	Pd a quart of sack given a Minister..	0	1	4
	Pd for soulder to Wm Mountford to mend the leads of the steeple	1	0	0
	Pd for Beere & suger for Coll. Morgan,† Capt. Juel, Mr Hussey	0	17	2
	for putting out the kings armes	0	0	10
	Pd Jo: Weaver for the Communion table & other work done in the Chappell	0	6	6
	Pd for a pass book for the Townes use	0	2	6
	Pd for frankincense & brimston to burne in the Chappell.	0	1	0
	Pd for 2 pairs of hinges for 2 seat dores in the Chappell & for mending a seat broke when the Soldiers were there	0	1	6

* Hartlebury Castle was strengthened by Captain Sandys, but surrendered in two days without firing a shot.—*Nash*, i., 568.

† The Parliamentary leader who took Hartlebury Castle May 16, 1646.

1651-2	Pd my ptner Burlton as he paid for a prsent sent to my lord Wile	01	05	0
1651-3	The second of September paid for ringing for the rooting of the Scotts by Mr Bailiffs order * ..	00	05	0
1654-5	Recd ye Stipend for ye Chappell out of the Rectory of Ombersley by the hands of Mr Greene at Michaelmas 1655	8	0	0
	To the wid. Monox when ye scollers broke up her wine..	0	2	8
	To John Weaver for a frame Joyned to the pue to hold a Bason to baptise Infants	00	01	2
	Pd Mr Oasland by the Townes order for Mich 1658 1 yeare	60	00	00
	Pd for wyne sent to Mr Lyttleton at Mr Bayliffs house ..	00	03	08
1657-8	Sept. 11 pd sweepinge the prke against the pclamur of Lord Richard protector	00	00	08
	Pd 5 men that carryed the halberts at pclamacn	00	03	06
	Pd the Trumpeter by the Tounes order	00	05	00
	Pd Will Brodhurst making pulpit cushyn, plush for the Cushin 18*s*. fronge & tasles & skins &c.	01	14	08
1658-9	Pd ye widdow Monox for wine & beare when ye Lord ptector was pclamed	03	16	0
	For Beare Wine & fagotts when yt bardgmen weare examined yt travelled on ye Lords Day	0	4	4
	Pd Setting up Kinges Arms for the Chappell	2	10	0
1660	12 May 1660 paid for wine & beare at the pclayminge the king	06	03	00
	for 4 qrts of sack for 4 ministers that preched	00	06	08
	31 July for meate at Mr ffolys venson eating	05	02	07
1661-2	Pd to Peter Rea for fetching the laxe lane bridge at Redstone	0	1	10
1663	Given to the ringers when the Lord Windsor came thorough the Toune	0	2	6
	Pd at the eating of Sr Henry Herberts venison in wine ..	00	19	4
	Pd for 6 gallons of wt wine wch was sent to the Lord Windsor	01	00	0
	Spent treatinge with the Curryer	00	00	7
	Recd of Thomas Hinks & Josh Knight for their freedome	08	00	0

[In a fly-leaf at the end of the book are the names of those that furnished arms. The arms furnished were 38 muskets, 3 halberds, 2 calivers, 3 corslets, 3 fowling pieces, 2 pistols, a pike, and a lance.]

* Dunbar.

From other Corporation Account Books of later date are gathered the following:—

1709 Paid for playing ye engines & taking them in ye Church again 0 3 0

Recd of Mr Sam. Slade for a seate in ye Chancel for the Lives of Mrs Jone Baker his daughter & Mrs Susanna Nash his grand daughter £1 0 0

1753 Sir George Lyttelton gave £100 to the town which was to be spent in applying for an Act of Parliament for the New Road to Cleobury & Kinlet.

1780 A list of tolls to be taken at Bewdley Hop Market.

£25 is to be allowed the Bailiff towards the expence of the Bailiff's Feast.

1799 Whereas the price of Liquor &c. is increased the Bailiff is to be allowed £52 10*s*. per ann.

1807 Miles Peter Andrewes M.P. gives £1000 to the Town.

1808 Miles Peter Andrewes M.P. gives £2000 to the Town.

1808 The Guildhall [standing on the S.W. side of the chapel] and the buildings round the church are to be taken down.

1817 Mr William Turton of Wribbenhall is going to take legal steps to reduce the number of Inns in conformity with the Charter.

1822 The rooms over the gateway in Welch gate, and a house adjoining, are to be purchased for £160—then to be pulled down & thrown into the road.

1831 Doglane Gateway is to be removed.

[Slade Baker, Esq., of Sandbourne, signed the order for its removal, and John Clarke helped to take it down. Both are still living.]

1830-1-2 Paid for clothing the bellman £50 17 0

Bailiffs of Bewdley.

1660 Thomas Wootton
1661 Thomas Dedicott
1662 John Grove
1663 William Longmore
1664 Thomas Burlton
1665 Peter Walter
1666 William Watmore
1667 Edd Longmore (dd. in office)
William Dedicott
1668 John Clare
1669 Timothy Wright
1670 Henry Sandals
1671 John Bury
1672 Peter Branch
1673 Samuel Moore
1674 Joseph Pooler
1675 Thomas Poole
1676 Thomas Watmore
1677 John Soley
1678 Thomas Burlton
1679 Peter Walter
1680 William Dedicott
1681 John Clare
1682 John Bury
1683 Peter Branch
1684 Joseph Pooler
1685 Thomas Watmore
1686 Adam Littleton
1687 Francis Hale
1688 Edward Best
1689 Francis Vicaris
1690 Humphrey Yarranton
1691 Thomas Burlton
1692 Samuel Slade
1693 Thomas Burlton, grocer
1694 Thomas Walter
1695 James Compson
1696 Richard Clare
1697 Nicholas Ward
1698 Simon Wood
1699 Bonham Caldwall
1700 Samuel Hackluit
1701 Joseph Tyndall, mercer
1702 Samuel Slade
1703 Edward Best
1704 Thomas Burlton, grocer
1705 Thomas Walter
1706 Bonham Caldwall
1707 Thomas Smith (under the old charter)
Samuel Slade (under the new charter)
1708 John Rock (under the old charter)
James Compson (under the new charter)
1709 Nicholas Ward
1710 Joseph Tyndall
1711 Samuel Slade
1712 Nicholas Ward
1713 James Compson
1714 Nicholas Ward
1715 William Wood
1716 Thomas Penn

1717 William Wood
1718 Nicholas Ward
1719 Thomas Cheeke
1720 Joseph Pardoe
1721 William Dix
1722 John Hayley
1723 Thomas Meysey
1724 James Compson
1725 Richard Jones
1726 Adam Prattinton
1727 Robert Yarranton
1728 Richard Hincksman
1729 Nicholas Ward
1730 John Prattinton
1731 Thomas Cheeke
1732 Robert Yarranton
1733 John Hayley
1734 Richard Jones
1735 Adam Prattinton
1736 Robert Yarranton
1737 William Crump
1738 Robert Yarranton
1739 Richard Jones
1740 Nehemiah Jeavens
1741 Robert Yarranton
1742 Thomas Cheeke
1743 John Hayley (died in office)
Robert Yarranton
1744 Richard Jones
1745 Adam Prattinton
1746 Richard Hincksman
1747 Joseph Crane
1748 Benjamin Best
1749 Adam Prattinton
1750 Richard Jones
1751 Adam Prattinton
1752 Thomas Brookholding
1753 Joseph Radnall
1754 Joseph Sheward
1755 The Rev. Butler Cowper
1756 The Rev. Thomas Howard
1757 John Hayley
1758 John Ingram, sen.
1759 Adam Prattinton
1760 John Ingram
1761 Thomas Prattinton
1762 Thomas Cheeke
1763 Joseph Radnall
1764 Joseph Crane
1765 John Patten
1766 Adam Prattinton
1767 John Crane
1768 Wilson Aylesbury Roberts
1769 James Fryer
1770 Nathaniel Adey
1771 William Prattinton
1772 Wilson Aylesbury Roberts
1773 John Crane
1774 Joseph Sheward
1775 James Prattinton
1776 Nathaniel Adey
1777 John Crane
1778 Samuel Kenrick
1779 Samuel Skey
1780 Nathaniel Adey
1781 James Fryer
1782 William Prattinton
1783 Nathaniel Adey
1784 Thomas Sheward
1785 John Glover
1786 Joseph Crane
1787 Thomas Baker
1788 Joseph Crane
1789 John Glover
1790 Jonathan Skey
1791 Samuel Baker
1792 James Fryer
1793 Thomas Howard Crane
1794 Thomas Baker
1795 Jonathan Skey
1796 Joseph Crane
1797 Samuel Baker
1798 Jonathan Skey
1799 Samuel Baker
1800 James Fryer
1801 Thomas Howard Crane
1802 Thomas Baker
1803 Jonathan Skey
1804 Joseph Crane
1805 Samuel Baker
1806 Jonathan Skey
1807 Rev. Edward Baugh
1808 James Fryer

1809 Wilson Aylesbury Roberts, jun.
1810 Thomas Howard Crane
1811 Joseph Crane
1812 Wilson Aylesbury Roberts
1813 George Baker
1814 Joseph Seager
1815 Wilson Aylesbury Roberts
1816 James Fryer
1817 Thomas Howard Crane
1818 Joseph Crane
1819 John Brookholding
1820 Robert Pardoe
1821 Thomas Cartwright
1822 Thomas Pilkington
1823 Rev. Joseph Crane
1824 Thomas Shaw
1825 George Baker
1826 John Brookholding
1827 Thomas Pilkington
1828 John Williams
1829 Thomas Howard Crane
1830 James Fryer
1831 Thomas Sheward Cartwright
1832 Thomas Sheward Cartwright
1833 Thomas Cartwright
1834 Slade Baker

MAYORS.

1835 Slade Baker
1836 John Bury
1837 John Nichols
1838 John Beddoe
1839 James Cole
1840 William Bucklee
1841 Thomas Sheward Cartwright
1842 George Baker
1843 James Holder
1844 Joseph Farmer
1845 George Masefield
1846 Thomas Townley Lancaster
1847 James Banks
1848 Adam Prattinton
1849 John Baker
1850 John Bury
1851 Slade Baker
1852 John Beddoe
1853 Christopher Piggott Bancks
1854 Christopher Piggott Bancks
1855 James Cole
1856 John Wildman Thomas Lea
1857 Thomas Owens
1858 John Nicholls
1859 James Tart
1860 John Nicholls
1861 John Reeve
1862 John Reeve
1863 John Gabb
1864 Thomas Owens
1865 Alfred Maurice Clinch
1866 Robert Williams
1867 William Hawkes Ryland
1868 Whittington Landon
1869 Whittington Landon
1870 John Nicholls
1871 Thomas Owens
1872 Benjamin Gardner
1873 William Nichols Marcy
1874 William Nichols Marcy
1875 Whittington Landon
1876 Charles Pountney
1877 Robert Acton Pardoe
1878 { Robert Acton Pardoe (to May 5, 1879)
William Nichols Marcy }
1879 Samuel Jefferies
1880 Samuel Jefferies
1881 William Nichols Marcy
1882 Whittington Landon

Members of Parliament for Bewdley.

12 James I. Thomas Edmunds
18 ,, Thomas Edmunds (Treasurer of the Household)
21 ,, Ralph Clare
1625 Ralph Clare
1626 Ralph Clare
1628 Sir Ralph Clare, Knight of the Bath
1640 Sir Henry Herbert, Kt.
1640 Sir Henry Herbert, Kt.
1647 William Hopkins (died before taking his seat)
1658-9 Edward Pitts of Kyre
1660 Thomas Foley the elder
1661 Sir Henry Herbert (d. 1673)
1673 Thomas Foley the elder *
1676 Henry Herbert
1679 Philip Foley
1680 Philip Foley
1685 Sir Charles Lyttelton
1689 (Convention) Henry Herbert
1690 Henry Herbert †
1694 Salwey Winnington
1695 Ditto
1698 Ditto
1700 Salwey Winnington
1702 Ditto
1705 Ditto
1708 Hon. Henry Herbert ‡
1709 Charles Cornwall
1710 Anthony Lechmere (unseated)
1710 Salwey Winnington
1713 Grey James Grove
1714 Grey James Grove
1717 Crewe Offley
1720 Ditto
1722 Ditto
1725 Ditto
1727 Ditto
1734 William Bowles
1734 Phineas Bowles
1741 William Bowles
1747 William Bowles (d. 1748)
1748 William Lyttelton
1754 William Lyttelton §
1755 Right Hon. William Finch
1761 Sir Edward Winnington
1762 Sir Edward Winnington ||
1768 The Hon. Thomas Lyttelton (unseated)

---

* Unseated in 1676.
† Created Lord Herbert, April, 1694; d. 1709.
‡ Second Lord Herbert; succ. 1709; d. 1738.
§ Made Governor of South Carolina.
|| Re-elected on being made Storekeeper of the Ordnance.

1769 Sir Edward Winnington
1774 William Henry Lyttelton*
1777 Lord Westcote (re-elected as Lord of the Treasury)
1780 Lord Westcote (of Ireland)
1784 Lord Westcote
1790 Hon. George ffulke Lyttelton
1796 Miles Peter Andrewes
1802 Ditto
1806 Ditto
1807 Ditto
1812 Ditto (died 1814, ætat. 72)
1814 Charles Edward Wilson
1819 Wilson Aylesbury Roberts
1820 Ditto
1826 Ditto
1830 Ditto
1831 Ditto
1832 Sir Thomas Edward Winnington
1835 Sir T. E. Winnington
1837 Ditto
1841 Ditto
1847 Thomas James Ireland
1848 William Drogo Montagu, Viscount Mandeville
1852 Sir Thomas Edward Winnington
1857 Ditto
1859 Ditto
1865 Ditto
1868 Sir Richard Attwood Glass (unseated)
1869 John Cunliffe Pickersgill Cunliffe (unseated)
1869 Major the Hon. Augustus H. A. Anson
1874 Charles Harrison
1880 Charles Harrison (unseated)
1880 Enoch Baldwin

High Stewards of Bewdley.

1606 Sir Robert Steward, Knt.
1708 Hon. Henry Herbert, afterwards Lord Herbert of Cherbury
1738 William Bowles, Esq.
1753 Sir George Lyttelton, afterwards created Lord Lyttelton
1773 Thomas 2nd Lord Lyttelton
1779 Wm. Henry Lord Westcote, created Lord Lyttelton
1808 George Fulke 2nd Lord Lyttelton
1828 William Henry 3rd Lord Lyttelton
1837 George William 4th Lord Lyttelton
1876 Charles George 5th Lord Lyttelton

* Afterwards Lord Westcote: his portrait hangs in Bewdley Town-hall.

Recorders of Bewdley.

[1616] Sir Francis Eure
[1621] Sir James Whitlocke
[1625-58] Edward Littleton
[1670] Sir Timothy Lyttelton, Kt.
1670 Thomas Powys, Serjeant-at-Law
1671 Sir Thomas Walcot, Kt., M.P., of Bitterley Court
1685 Henry Townsend
1688 John Soley
1710 John Hoo, Serjeant-at-Law
1716 John Soley
1720 Henry Lord Herbert
1738 William Bowles
1745 John Soley
1775 Charles Baldwyn
1780 William Henry Lord Westcote
1808 John Knight of Wolverley

Deputy Recorders.

1633 — Hayles
Car. II. Leonard Sympson
1683 John Soley
1686 Henry Toye
1708 Samuel Hunt
1727 Thomas Manning
1752 William Crump
1756 John Cowper
1775 Wilson Aylesbury Roberts
1809 Samuel Baker
1816 Slade Baker
1833 William Nichols Marcy

Town Clerks.

1833 William Nichols Marcy
1873 Richard Hemingway

Borough Treasurers.

1835 Robert Acton Pardoe
1876 Robert Henry Whitcombe

Copy of the Charter of Edward the Fourth

Constituting Bewdley a Free Borough

A.D. 1472.

EDWARDUS Dei gr'a Rex Anglie Francie et Dominus Hibernie Om'ibus ad quos presentes l're p'venerint salutem. Sciatis qd ad humilem supplicaco'em Dilecor' ligeor' n'ror' Burgensium et Inh'itancium Ville n're de Beaudeley ac ob certas consideraco'es nos specialiter moventes de gr'a nostra speciali ac ex certa sciencia et mero motu n'ris concessimus et p' presentes concedimus pro nobis et heredib' n'ris quantum in nobis est qd villa n'ra predc'a cum precinctu eiusdem liber burgus sit in p'pet'm et de Burgensib' eiusdem ville et precinctus eiusdem in p'pet'm sit corporata et qd iidem Burgenses et successores sui Burgenses ville illius et precinctus eiusdem sic corporati sint una Co'itas p'petua corporat' in re et in no'i'e per nomen Burgensium ville de Beaudeley et precinct' eiusdem h'eantq' successionem p'petuam ac co'e sigillum p' negociis suis d'cam villam et precinctum eiusdem concernent' deservitur' in p'petu'm Et qd iidem Burgenses et successores sui p' idem nomen sint p'sone habiles et capaces in lege et qd ip'i et successores sui terras et tenementa redditus servitia et reversiones quecumq' a quacumq' persona sive quibuscumq' personis ea eis dare concedere legare vel assignare volente seu volentib' perquirere possint habend' et tenend' eisdem Burgensib' et successorib' suis in p'petu'm. Et ulterius in relevamen eor'dem Burgensium et successor' suor' de ulteriori gratia nostra concessimus et p' presentes concedimus eisdem Burgensib' et successorib' suis qd quilibet Burgensium predictor' pro tempore existen' sit quietus per totum et infra regnum nostrum Anglie et potestatem n'ram de thelonio pontagio passagio paiagio lestagio tronagio ancoragio stallagio caragio pesagio panagio terragio picagio chiminagio muragio fossagio pedagio kaiagio et de om'ibus aliis consuetudinib' de et pro om'ibus bonis et mercandisis suis in om'ibus locis infra regnum et potestatem n'ra predicta tam per terram q'm per mare et aquam dulcem in p'petu'm. Eo qd expressa mencio de vero valore annuo premissor' vel alicuius eor' in presentibus minime facta existat Aut aliquo statuto actu sive ordinatione incontrarium facto edito sive ordinato Aut aliqua re causa vel materia quacumque non obstante In cuius rei testimonium has l'ras nostras fieri fecimus patentes.

Teste me ip'o apud Westm' vicesimo die Octobris Anno regni nostri duodecimo p' l're de privato sigillo et de data prela auctoritate parliamenti.

Extracts from Dowles Parish Registers, &c.

REGISTRUM PAROCHIALE DE DOWLES.

[Vol. I. parchment 1572 to 1641.]

Johannes filius Will'mi Grove et Joannæ uxoris ejus baptizatus fuit xxiiit.o Novembris 1572.

1596 The vith day of Januarye was buried Joice Angels a stranger travelinge to Bottrells Aston wheare shee was borne.

The xxth day of May was maried Jhon Trowe and Mary Hariots by vertue of a lycence.

1608 Jocosa filia Humfredi Garmeston et Jocosæ uxoris ejus baptizata fuit decimo die Julii anno supradicto.

1610 This year Mr Thomas Haward bestowed a Beere upon this Church being made at his only cost and Chardge 14 Aprill.

Morgan Lewis peregrinus sepultus fuit xxmo die ffebr. et dedit per Voluntatem suam pauperibus huius parochiæ—xs.

1610 Thomas Weaver de la Boate Loade obiit xxiiitio die ffebr.

1612 Thomas Haward generosus obiit decimo quarto die Julii et sepultus fuit decimo quinto die Julii; qui dum vixit multa bona et præclara huic parochiæ fecit.

1617 xx Jan. Robert of the green load* was buried.

1619 Eliseus . . . . . licenced by John L Byshop of Norwich preached at Dowlls the xxvth feb.

Mr Hamonds† the 1 of May.

Mr Wright‡ the xviith of August.

Mr Stanway the 4 of January.

1631 The 27th of Novemb. was baptised Francis the son of Griffin ap Owen & Elizabeth his wife.

---

* The Green Load was close to the "Folly Ford," where Dowles borders on Upper Arley.

† Rector of Ribbesford.

‡ Minister of Bewdley chapel.

1659 At this meeting it is resolved by ye Parishioners yt evy Com'unicant Parish. shall pay for bread & wine pence a peece.

[The above item is extracted from entries in a paper memorandum book.]

(Book No. 3.)

This Register Book was bought in ye yeare 1656.

In 1657 there were 5 marriages; in 1658, 35.
1659 " " 36 " ; 1660, 31.
1661 " " 1 " ; 1662, 0.

1669 ffrancis Ap owen was buried Jan. 17th.

1674 Thomas Billingsley of Bromigham married Aug. 4th.

1683 Job Walker Esq. of Wotton and Rebecca the second daughter of Tho: Ld ffolliot of Mitton in the parish of Kederminster were married August the 23rd.

Oct. 7 1695

Memorand. that whereas Mary ye wife of Tho: Hale of ye Boat Load claimed ye upper kneeling in ye Seat belonging yt, the Hill House & some others: the parties grieved consenting to refer ye contraversie to ye Right Honourable Henry Lord Herbert, his Lordship was pleased upon ye hearing of ye evidence to determine yt ye upper kneeling belonged to ye Hill House, & ordered this his determination should be here entered by me.

NATH. WILLIAMS, Rector.

Some Collections in Dowles Church.

Collected ffeb. 28: 1685 toward the Repayre of houses burnt at Hereford two shillings & twopence.

June 15, 1686 toward ye Releif of ye ffrench Protestants yt fled to England 11s 6d (By 35 subscribers.)

A Collection in the pish of Dowles towards ye rebuilding of St Pauls Church in the citty of London Anno 1678:—11s 2d

The names of the Contributors towards the Redemption of those taken by the Turk 1680—9s 2d

June 1681 towards the repayre of St Albans steeple .. 0 02 7

Nov. 6, 1681 for lesser poland 2s 2d

1687 Towards the releif of the Irish protestants—14s 10½d

Collected in April 5, 1699 towards the Relife of the french prodistons 01 14 09

1703 March 5 for ye Inhabitants of ye Principality of Orange forced to quit their native country for ye sake of Religion to ye number of three thousand .. .. 0 9 8 (s d)

1704 June 18 for ye Reliefe of ye distressed Widows & Orphans of those Seamen & Mariners who lost their lives in ye dreadful Storm & Tempest which happened on ye 26th—27th. days of 9ber last past 14s 3d

1708	May 30 for Bewdley in the County of Worcester ..	4s	9¼d
	Jan. 30 ye Head of the Cannon Gate at Edinburgh in North Britain	3s	2d
1709	Ju 19 for St Mary Redcliffe Church in Bristol	3s	8d
1706	xbr 22 for Darlington Church in ye County Palatine of Durham	5s	7¼d
1709	Nov. 22 for ye Poor Palatines	11s	11d
1715/16	Jan. 16 Collected the Cow Breif from House to House ..	4s	1d
1716/17	March 11 for ye Reformed Episcopall Churches in Poland & Polish Prussia	1s	4d
1723	for ye Brief of Brighthelmston in Com. Sussex occasioned by ye overflowing of ye Sea. May ye 6th	2s	4d
1729	March 24 for ye Protestants of Copenhagen	1s	1d
1739	Aug. 6 for ye Brief of Bobi & Villar in ye Valley of Luzerne in Peidmont	0s	9½d
1742	May 17 for ye Oyster Dredgers in Com. of Kent.. ..	0s	2d
1744	June 10 for ye Brief of Bewdley Chapel in Com. of Worcester	0s	0d
1756	7ber 13 for Clunn Church in Com. of Salop	2s	0d
1757	7ber 5 for Brighthelmstone Fortifications in Com. Essex	1s	1½d
1762	July 28 for Saarbruck Ch. and School in Germany ..	7s	2d
1763	June 30 for ye Colleges in America	14s	0d
1765	March 17 for ye Philippen Colony in Turkish Moldavia.	2s	3d
1768	Aug. 15 for ye Voudois Protestants..	2s	7½d
1770	May 14 for ye Brief of Dowles Church in Com. of Salop	5s	0d
1772	April 7 for Inundations in Com. Salop	0s	2d

[In all about one thousand collections by Brief are registered, filling 70 folio pages.]

In Dowles Overseers' and Churchwardens' Accounts.

Spent at ye Boat load when company met about ye foxes. 00 00 1½

Mr Nath. Williams late Rector of Dowles (who died Aug. 12, 1701) left five pounds unto ye Poor of ye said Parish the interest thereof to be laid out in buying some of ye Books hereafter named, viz., Bibles, Common Prayer with ye New Testamt, Expositions upon ye Church Catechism, & Helps to Com'unicants, Christian Monitor, Wake upon death, or such like—to be distributed every 2nd year by Rector.

1701	Spent at ye Bull (at Mr Price's Induction)..	0	04	0
	Paid for Ringing on Novemb. ye 5th 1s 2d & for drink at ye Bonfire 2s 6d	0	03	8
1704	for Ringing when ye joyful News was brought of ye glorious Victory obtain'd by ye Duke of Marlborough over ye ffrench at Hochstet	0	0	6

1706 To Will. Grove for a journey to Bridgnorth to pay in the money for windows 0 2 6

to John Lucas Collector of Money for Births & Burials, to pay in ye Money 0 2 6

A journey to Bridgenorth about pressing Soldiers .. 0 02 6

An Account of Gommer Perks's Goods which were apprised by Thomas Weaver churchwarden & John Lucas Sept. 2, 1706 as follows

One Wheel 0 01 6

One high crown hat & hat case 6d 0 00 6

&c. &c. &c. £. s. d. q.

1707 ffor Urchins 0 00 8 0

ffor Vagabonds 0 02 8 0

ffor a Hue & Cry 0 00 6 0

1710 ffor 30 Urchins 5s 0d

ffor mending the Dyall.. .. .. 11s 0d

1716 ffor goeing with two vaggabons to Areley 1s 0d

ffor goeing to Button Bridge to pay Bridge money .. 1s 10d

1735 For three foxes 0 3 0

(Book No. 4)

This Booke was bought in May 1698 By Francis Radnall. Price 10s.

This Register is surveyed till March 25, 1698 by Joh. Yapp survr. Nath: Williams, Rector.

1701 Nathaniel Williams Rector of this parish dyed August ye 12.

1702 Sept. 24. Edward Bury of Stanford in Com. Wigorn Bachelour & Anne Postunne of Upper Areley in Com. Staffordiæ Spinster were married. License.

At foot of page "Exd by Tho: Davies, Surveyr."

1716 Bap. Apr. 15th. Joseph son of John Tunkes Pattinringmaker.

1720 Jan. 3 Samuel Hassal Physician & Apothecary of Bewdley.

1724 The Reverend Mr Martin Crane junier Buried October ye 28th.

1760 Aug. 31 Mary daughter of Joseph Morris a viper came into bed to her & bit her, which caused her death.

1795 May 30 Pd Mr Hide of Stottesdon for Dowles share of the Man to serve in his Majesty's Navy £2 2 0

1803 23 Aug. Taking Account of all the Live Stock Waggons Carts & Draft Horses in the Parish.

Puting down all the Peopil in the Parish in thair Different Classes Liable to surve in the Armey in case of Invasion.

Pedigree of Mortimer of Wigmore.

Lords of Bewdley.

Ralph de Mortimer (i.) = Milicent

Hugh de Mortimer (i) Lord of Wigmore d. Feb. 26, 1181 = Maud d. of William Longespée, Duke of Normandy

(1) Milicent d. of . . . Ferrers, Earl of Derby = Roger de Mortimer (i) d. June 24, 1214 = (2) Isabel sister and heir of Hugh de Ferrers of Oakham and Lechlade, d. *circa* 1252

Hugh de Mortimer (ii) d. 1227. s.p. = Annora d. of William de Braose

Ralph de Mortimer (ii) 5th Lord of Wigmore, d. Aug. 6, 1246 = Gladuse d. of Llewellyn Pr. of Wales

Roger de Mortimer (ii) d. Oct. 27, 1282 = Maud dr. & co-heir of Wm. de Braose of Brecknock, d. 1301

Hugh de Mortimer of Chelmarsh, d. 1273

Edmund de Mortimer (i), b. on or before 1255; a Clerk in 1263; d. 1304 = Margaret d. of Sir Wm. de Fendles (a Spaniard)

Roger Mortimer (iii), Earl of March, born April 25, 1287; executed Nov. 29, 1328 = Joan d. and heir of Sir Peter de Geneville, born Feb. 2, 1286; died 1356

Isolda (heiress of Upper Arley) = (1) Walter de Balun; (2) Hugh de Audley

Edmund Mortimer (ii) d. Dec., 1331 = Elizabeth d. of Bartholomew Lord Badlesmere

Roger Mortimer (iv) Earl of March b. 1328; d. Feb. 26, 1360 = Philippa d. of William de Montacute, Earl of Salisbury, d. Jan. 3, 1382

Edmund Mortimer (iii) Earl of March and Ulster d. 1381 = Philippa d. and heir of Lionel Duke of Clarence

Roger Mortimer (v) Earl of March slain in Ireland 1398 = Alianor d. of Thomas Holland, Duke of Kent

Anne d. of Edmund Earl of Stafford, d. 1433 = Edmund Mortimer (iv) Earl of March, d. 1425. s.p.

Anne Mortimer = Richard E. of Cambridge, behead. 1415

Richard, Duke of York slain at Wakefield 1460 = Cecilie d. of Ralph Nevill, Earl of Westmoreland, d. 1495

Edward Earl of March, who became King EDWARD IV.

Miscellanea.

N the forest near Button Oak about 100 years ago a gold coin of the Emperor Tiberius was found. On one side was TI CAEAP DIVI AVG F AVGVSTVS; on reverse, a figure sitting with a spear holding a branch of olive, PONTIF MAXIMVS.

A tree of great interest to botanists was growing till lately in Wyre Forest. It was a "Sorb Tree" (*Pyrus domestica*), and was the only apparently wild tree of the species in Britain. It was mentioned in the *Philosophical Transactions* for 1678 by Alderman Pitts, of Worcester, and was considered an old tree at that time. It was burnt down by some miscreant in 1862. Illustrations of the tree are given in *Nash* (vol. i., page 10) and in Lees' *Botany of Worcestershire* (pages xci. and 4). George Jorden traced out what he thought to be the ruins of a hermitage near the spot.

"A strange and true Relation of a Young Woman possest with the Devill By name Joyce Dovey dwelling at Bewdley neer Worcester. With a particular of her actions & how the evill Spirit speakes within her giving fearful answers unto those Ministers and others that come to discourse with her. As it was certified in a letter from Mr. James Dalton unto Mr. Th. Groom Ironmonger over against Sepulchres Church in London. Imprinted at London 1647." This is the title of a book of which only two printed copies are known to be

G

now in existence. Dr. Prattinton's MSS. contain a written copy of the whole; but it is only of interest as showing the superstition of the age. Dovie or Dovey was a common name in Bewdley at the time mentioned; and the Rev. John Boraston, Rector of Ribbesford, was one of the ministers who visited her.

Susan Wowen, of Bewdley, had horns 3 inches long at the back of her head, which were shed every three years. In all she shed about 8 or 9. Mr. Soley, of Sandbourne, had one of them tipped with silver; and another was sent to Oxford. Tradition relates that she was a very wicked woman. Dr. Prattinton collected all the information he could obtain from ancient and modern history about people similarly circumstanced, and the results fill many closely-written pages of his MSS.

Winterdyne House was built by Sir Edward Winnington about 1760. Richard Symonds, who accompanied Charles I. in the civil wars (1644), says in his diary that there was then a "grotto cut out of the quarry of stone within Ticknell parke towards the Severne."

The Rev. Walter Sweeper (see page 22) was buried at Stroud June 9, 1636. He published a discourse on Prov. xii., 16, and another on "Israel's Redemption by Xt, Wherein is confuted the Arminian Vniversall Redemption." From the preface to this book we learn that the famous Countess of Pembroke was a native of Bewdley. He says, "I intended to dedicate this to your truly noble sister the late deceased Countesse of Pembrock, in token of my thankfulnesse for her continuall favours shewed ever since she and my Lord her husband placed me in Bewdley where she first drew her happie breath; which place of her birth is styled by an ancient Poet, *Delitium rerum bellus locus.*"* (See page 4.)

The old sign-board of the "Cock and Pye" Inn is very interesting to students of Shakspere, and has often been engraved.

* Gloucestershire *Notes and Queries*, part xii.

Index.

www.ingramcontent.com/pod-product-compliance
Lightning Source LLC
Chambersburg PA
CBHW020229030726
47497CB00009B/3019

* 9 7 8 3 3 3 7 4 2 9 0 7 2 *